Wildfowl Carving MAGAZINE

OLD-SCHOOL DECOYS

CARVING AND PAINTING TRADITIONAL WATERFOWL FROM THE PAST

Keith Hendrickson

CONTENTS

INTRODUCTION

It was the early '80s, I was finishing up college, and had a bad itch for duck hunting. My high school buddy's dad had just started a duck hunting club on the Core Sound in North Carolina. It was an upscale club, and a few of the members brought some locally carved decoys to decorate the lodge. The club was just a couple of miles from the local school that hosted a small carving group making up what became known as the Core Sound Decoy Carvers Guild.

This guild began holding a decoy festival that drew carvers and collectors from all over the East Coast. It was at these shows that I began noticing the different carving styles coming from various regions of the continent. I met many of the local carvers and collectors and drooled over some outrageously expensive decoys in some of those collections.

It didn't take long with my near empty wallet that I realized there was no realistic way I could afford to have a nice decoy collection. I really appreciated the old-looking blocks, and when I had them in hand—examining their rough carvings, the worn-off paint, their simplistic designs—I could drift off and imagine their history and the hunts that had been had over them.

I decided that if I wanted some of these old-looking blocks to enjoy and hunt over, I would have to learn how to carve them myself, using what little woodworking skill I had. They would be accurate to their carving school and history, and down the road I could admire them in hand and recall the hunts I had over them. Luckily, through the connections I have made over the years, I've been able to examine many notable historic decoys to pull patterns off of. These contacts were also more than willing to share their knowledge in the various regional carving schools to help direct me towards carving a very accurate block any hunter would be proud to have in their own rig.

In this book, five projects are presented featuring a bit of history from the carving school the design originated in. Each project includes patterns, step-by-step instructions, and close-up photos to guide the carver through the production and paint process. These projects will teach the carver skills used in laying up and creating any decoy from the most basic gunner to a nice shelf piece.

DELAWARE RIVER BLUEBILL

In this chapter, we will travel up the Delaware River into New Jersey to explore the decoy style that developed there. Along a 20-mile section between Delanco to Trenton, the hunters often used scull boats. They would set out their blocks in a likely area and then paddle the scull a hundred yards or so upwind. They would then wait until ducks decoyed into their blocks. Then the scull would begin, and they would slowly work their boat into the blocks, where they would flush and shoot the birds.

Delaware River decoys generally were more realistic than their cousins from up on the shore. They had more carved features, and the puddle ducks often had raised wingtips. The tail feathers were also cut in. Some carvers cut in grooves that suggested wing primaries on the backs of their divers. The river currents in the various areas often determined the cross-section shape of the decoy, which was more rounded below the waterline. Flat lead pad weights were nailed onto the bottoms instead of using inlaid lead or a weighted keel. Depending on the swiftness of the current, this weight was placed midway on the decoy or slightly back to raise the head and make the decoy ride the waves better. An offshoot of the Delaware River School was the John Blair School, developed by John Blair, Sr. (1842-1928). These blocks looked for the most part much the same as a Delaware River bird but were longer and leaner. Blair's decoys were probably modified to ride the water better in the areas he hunted.

When I began my research for this style, I got up with my buddy George Strunk to pick his brain. He quickly set me straight and said, "Look no further than John English, 1848-1915. He is the definition of the Delaware River School." Residing in Florence, New Jersey, he made decoys that were constructed much the same as the northern Jersey Shore decoys, using cedar or white pine bodies. The bodies were two halves, hollowed, and then nailed and caulked like their "Barnegat" counterparts. The heads were fairly narrow, often had tack eyes, and the bills had nostrils and other detail carved in.

John had two sons, Jack and Daniel. Both carved but Dan was a very prolific carver following in his father's footsteps. He eventually developed his own patterns, which were a good bit larger and stockier than his father's blocks. Larger birds became the trend; they were more visible for the numbers used in a set compared to the mostly life-sized birds John carved.

A selection of the hand tools used to re-create these masterworks.

A classic John English bluebill.

Coming up with a pattern (see page 27) for this project was a challenge. I had a good number of photographs off the internet of divers John English had carved, but none of the carvers I knew had a pattern I could use. I resolved the issue by using the photos I had available to draw out a pattern the approximate size of what the decoys would have been back in the day.

Ron Kobli, owner of the Decoys and Wildlife Gallery, allowed me to use a few photographs of a couple of original John English divers he had, and that allowed me to pull out some details to make this Delaware River Bluebill pattern and carving more accurate to the school style. For the most part, I will use all traditional hand tools to carve this bird. I'm not a big fan of using rotary carving tools because of all the dust they make, but you can certainly use whatever you are most comfortable using.

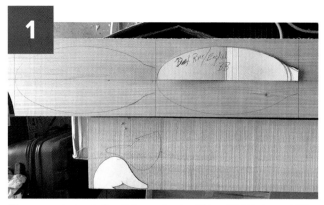

1

The wood stock for this project will be 2" thick and 6" wide white cedar. Draw the head pattern onto stock that is 1¾" to 2" thick. Make sure the grain of the wood runs straight down the bill to help prevent it from splitting. The body is 12" long, so I select a couple of boards that are fairly free of any knots that I can draw the body top profiles onto. Draw the top body profile onto both sides of each piece.

2

I decide which two inner sides of the boards should go together and then draw an oval about 1" inside the pattern lines. This will be where I will hollow out everything in that oval.

3

I set the two body pieces together on their sides, folding them together like a book so the inner-pattern comes together, and draw the side profile pattern onto the blocks.

4

I now draw inside the pattern an oval shape that will serve as a depth gauge for how much wood I can remove.

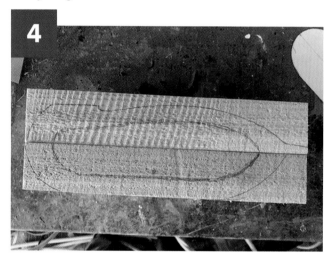

5

Around the outer edge of my oval, I drill in just to the thickness of the bit head since the outer part of the body will be rounded. As I move further in, I can drill out to the full depth of the tape mark.

6

I use a gouge to clean up the inside a bit and get more weight out of the block. A small bowl adze can also be used to hollow out the pieces.

7

A thick coat of Titebond III is put on both halves of the block. I let this soak in for about 15 minutes and then apply a bit more to one side. The two halves are clamped together, and the block is allowed to dry for 24 hours.

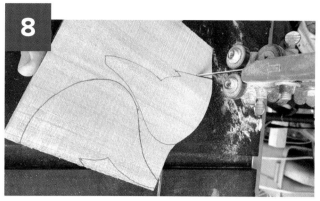

8

Moving on to the band saw, I cut my head pattern out. I usually cut out a pair of heads and will use the one I like the most. The second can be used if the head ever breaks down the road while hunting.

9

I begin cutting out the body on the saw. I only cut to about this point on each side, leaving uncut wood at the mid area of each side to help support the block when the side profile is cut.

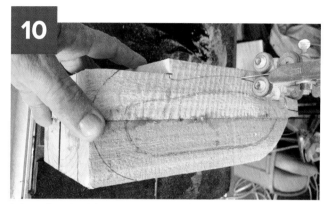

10

I then flip the block onto its side and completely cut out the side profile.

11

Once the side profile is cut, I flip the block back on its bottom and finish cutting out the middle of the side cuts. You can do this by eye or draw the cut in with a pencil.

12

Using a pencil, I draw an estimated waterline around the entire block. This will serve as the line I round the block up to from the bottom. I will use the seam line to round the back down to. I use a small block of wood to rest the pencil against while I turn the body around against the pencil. This line is approximately 1.5" up from the bottom.

13

I use a thin plastic ruler to mark a straight centerline around the body. The thin plastic will bend and take the shape of the body easily but still give me a straight line.

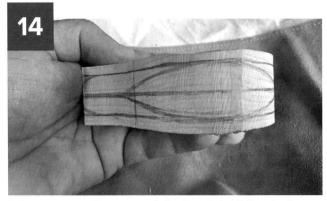

14

I draw a centerline around the head. A ½" line is drawn in on each side of the centerline. This will serve as the width of the top of the head and also the width of the bill (1" total). Draw in the crown of the head like this. This shape serves to help keep your carving symmetrical and doesn't have to be exact.

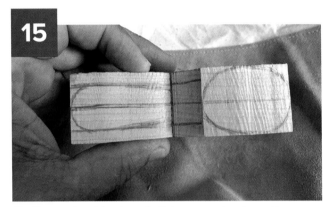

15

On the underside draw in this approximate pattern. The neck base will be rounded out and the bill width will be 1" total.

16

As I begin carving the head, I imagine a line approximately down the middle that shows which direction the grain of the wood will want to carve. Carving forward, I want to carve the front half. Carving to the back of the head, I need to carve back in that direction. If I get behind that line carving forward, the wood will want to split out. The same goes for carving the back of the head; get forward of the line carving back and the wood will want to split back. This tendency can actually be used to benefit the carving by removing wood faster, but be careful not to remove too much. If a chunk splits off, you can always use superglue and glue the piece back into place. Let the glue dry and continue carving.

17

I begin the carving at the bill margin line by making a series of stop cuts into each other to get to the bill width. This is done on each side of the bill.

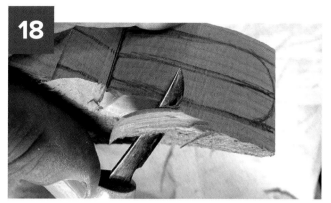

18

Once the margins are cut in, I can quickly remove the wood on each side of the bill to cut in the bill width. I do this on both sides and also flip the head over and remove wood along the sides of the bill looking at it from the top.

19

I round off the corners along the base of the neck. Again, I carve forward for the front two corners, and I carve to the back on the back two corners to prevent the wood from splitting off.

20

I make a deep stop cut about ¼" deep along the cheek line.

21

I carve into this stop cut, rounding the chin area into the cut. I also cut into the same cut from the base of the neck. Do this on both sides of the head to keep things symmetrical.

22

I begin to round out the crown of the head to the top lines I drew in at the beginning. Again, work on both sides of the head to keep things symmetrical.

23

Once I get the top of the head to its width, I round out the back of the head and neck.

24

Once both sides are rounded, look at the head from the back and top to check the symmetry.

25

Now that the back of the head and neck are rounded, I begin carving the front of the head and bill. I carve to my lines and avoid getting too close to the bottom of the bill.

26

Once both sides get to this point, I move back to finish rounding out the rest of the head. Both sides of the bill are fairly symmetrical at this point.

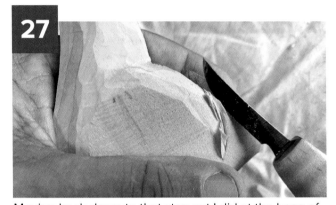

27

Moving back down to that stop cut I did at the base of the cheek and chin, I cut into the stop cut from both the cheek and the base of the neck. This is tapered back toward the back of the cheek.

28

This is how the cheek carving should end up on both sides of the head. This really sets off the roundness of the cheek, a feature John English was known for.

29

I draw in a line where the back of the bill margin will be on both sides.

30

I look at the bill from the top to make sure the curve in the drawn line is the same on both sides.

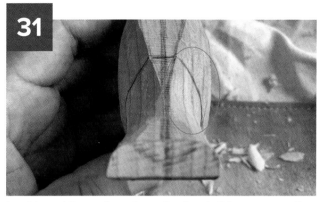

31

Looking at these lines from the front, things are pretty symmetrical, which is good. However, this line needs to look like it is not curved outward—it needs to look like it is straight.

32

The appearance of this drawn line is straightened from the front view by carving out the wood right in this area where the line is. Slowly remove wood on both sides of the bill, and redraw the curved line back in. Look at it again from the front and repeat the carving steps until that line appears to be straightened out from the front view.

33

Even though the line from the side view is curved, once the right amount of wood has been carved out, the line from the front view will appear nearly straight.

34

I draw in a small oval area where the eye channel will get carved in. Even though it is not a true channel, it will be more like a sunken valley area on both sides of the head.

35

This eye valley is carved in by cutting down from the top of the head to about where the eye will be and then carving up into that same area from the cheek.

36

I'm at the point where I can round out the end of the bill. I just want to get close to my lines to avoid making one side shaped differently than the other side.

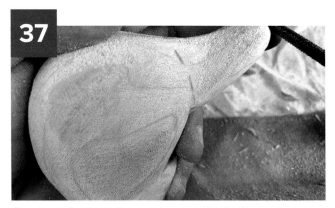

37

The head is ready for rasping out the knife marks and whatever band saw blade marks may be left on the head. At this point, I also use the rasp to finish rounding out the bill to ensure both sides have the same symmetrical curve.

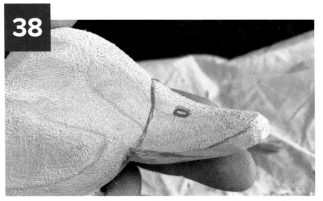

38

All of the bill detail that will be carved in is drawn in at this point. Make sure both sides appear symmetrical from both the front and top of the head.

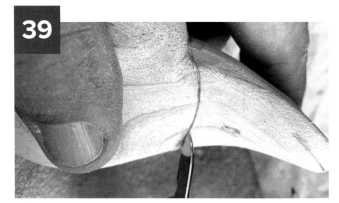

39

A small straight-edged detail knife is used to cut straight in along the bill margin line. The knife is razor sharp to ensure the wood cuts and doesn't pull the grain when coming over the harder dark grain.

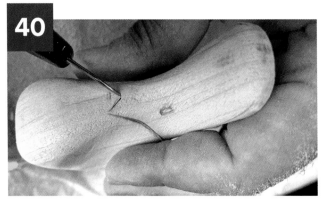

40

The V-notch at the top of the bill is also cut in using this same small knife.

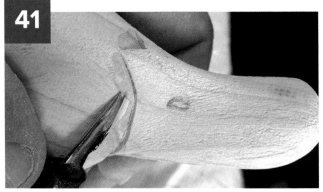

41

Switching to a small curved-point detail knife, I cut into the initial straight-in cut. I find that a curved blade slices into the straight-in cut much more smoothly.

42

Using the same curved-point detail knife, I cut in the bill detail at the front of the bill on both sides.

43

I cut in the lower mandible by cutting straight in along my bill line along the base of the upper mandible.

44

The lower mandible is finished by cutting up from the base of the lower mandible into the initial cut on the upper mandible. The back angled cut is also made.

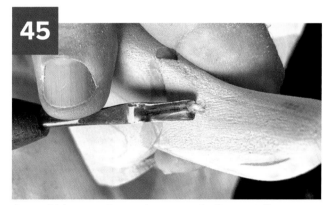

45

A small V-gouge is used to carve in the nostrils on both sides. It is easiest to carve this by cutting into the halfway point going forward, and then finishing the nostril by cutting back from the front part of the nostril. This prevents the cut from splitting as you try to work out of the cut.

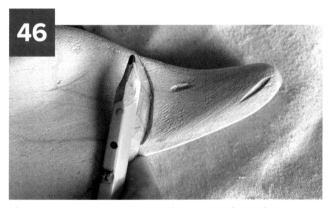

46

Using my pencil as a measuring gauge I get the approximate distance from the bottom of the bill to the top. I use my finger to set that distance.

47

Without moving my finger on the pencil, I use that same distance to mark in on the head from the top of the bill to about where I think the eye should be. This distance usually holds true for most ducks. I mark this distance on both sides of the head.

48

I then push a straight floral pin in on this mark on both sides.

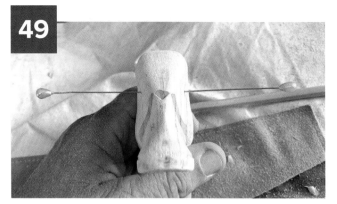

49

Looking at the pins straight on from the front, I adjust one side so it matches the horizontal imaginary line running through the head from one pin into the other.

50

I do this same thing looking at the pins from the top, adjusting the same chosen pin as needed.

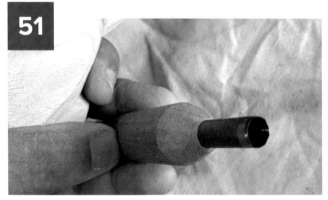

51

This is a homemade eye cut-in tool. It is a brass rifle cartridge that had the end cut, leaving the long part of the cartridge. It is approximately 9 mm in diameter. I stuck it into a drill and then ran the end of it against a piece of sandpaper to sharpen it. It is then glued into a piece of broom handle.

52

I carefully center the eye tool and press and rotate the tool so it cuts in about ⅛". Do this on both sides.

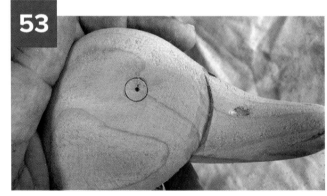

53

This is what I'm after. You can slightly twist the tool in place to make a mark and then adjust it if needed to center the pupil before actually cutting it in with the tool.

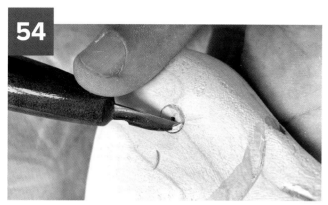

54

Using my small detail knife. I carefully cut in around what will be the pupil. I work my way around each eye.

56

Now that the head is finished, I place it onto the body, matching up the center lines. With my pencil, I draw an outline onto the body where the head sits.

58

I'll rough out the body using a small carving axe/hatchet. This will remove the shoulders of the block quickly. If you aren't comfortable using a hatchet, you can use a draw knife. I use a New Jersey-style carving bench for shaping the body. Note the removable chopping block that fits against the stop-block fixed to the bench.

55

This is the end result. This eye will fill nicely with paint to finish it off. Another eye option is to use 9 mm upholstery tacks. Tacks were usually what John English used, but I chose to cut these eyes in for this project.

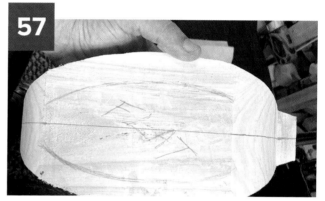

57

On the bottom of the decoy, I mark a line on each side about 1¼" in. When I start carving, I will try to stay on the outside of this line and round up from it to the waterline we marked earlier.

59

Holding the tail, I carefully look where I want my blade to hit and make small chops to remove the corner shoulders off the block. I rotate the block in my hand as I remove the wood until all four corners are somewhat rounded off. I then swap ends and do the same, removing the shoulder corners off the tail end of the block.

60

It looks rough, but in just about a minute, I have the bulk of the corners of the block all removed and ready for some draw knife work. Note that I stayed off the seam line and waterline as much as possible.

62

Be careful around the head shelf not to get too far into the head outline. It is better to stay a bit outside the line since the head will be carved into the body after a bit. By angling the drawknife, I can get in around the neck area closer than I could if I just used the knife perpendicular to the wood.

64

A "fair curve" or line along the side of a boat hull is one that is as smooth and symmetrical as it can be as it follows the path it must take. And so it is also with an old-school decoy. I check the fairness from the front view, side view, and tail view.

61

I remove the chopping block off my bench and trap the decoy body between my belly and the stop-block attached to the bench. I simply lean into the decoy to hold it in position. Using the drawknife as a push knife, I begin making more refined cuts to round out the shoulders of the block. Note that I like to hold my drawknife with the beveled edge down. By doing this, I can adjust the angle of the knife by rolling the bevel against the wood, cutting more or less wood while I push or pull the knife.

63

Once the body is pretty well rounded, I can refine its fairness using a spokeshave.

65

Time to glue the head onto the body. The neck will get carved into the body, so before either part is totally finished, the head is attached using the center lines to align the head so it is straight on the neck shelf. I use 5-minute epoxy for this task.

66

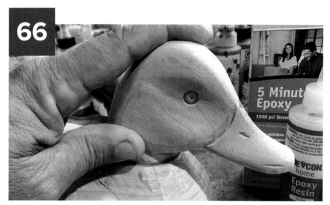

I apply a thin layer of epoxy on both the base of the head and the body's neck shelf. The head is positioned into place, and I then hold it, applying just pressure from the weight of my arm to hold it in place. Once the epoxy starts to set up, I can let go.

67

After letting the epoxy set up for about 15 minutes, but before it gets totally hard, I begin carving the neck into the body. I use several different knives for this depending on the section I am carving. For the back of the neck, I use my basic carving knife and cut straight down into the body. My goal is to carve out the seam between the head and body so there is no overlap from either part.

68

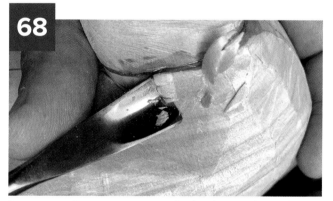

I use a small gouge to carve the body out along the side of the neck. This can be done with a knife, but it is difficult to make the knife's straight blade curve outward when carving.

69

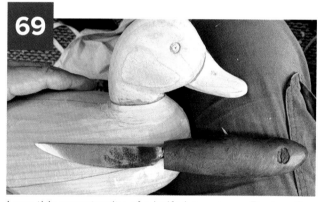

I use this monstrosity of a knife known as a Bushcraft Scandi to round out the breast of the body. This is the hardest area to carve since you basically have to carve against the grain of the wood. I noticed carver George Strunk used these large-bladed knives to carve in these hard-grained areas, and it appeared he carved these areas with little resistance. Unlike many other blade grinds, the Scandi grind runs to the edge with no angle change in what is also known as a zero grind. Scandi grinds have a flat section of the blade that starts at the tip of the bevel and runs to the spine. All of the best wood-carving knives use this same grind to have the least resistance to the wood; our smaller blades are just that—smaller compared to the much larger Scandi.

70

I use my thick-bladed Scandi to round out the breast of the bird and make sure all my lines are fair and symmetrical.

I like running a wooden dowel down through the decoy's head to prevent the neck from cracking and breaking off. I do not like using nails or screws because the neck can still crack if the head is hit hard. The screw will still hold it in place, but now you have a wobbly head to deal with. If the screw is run on the inside of the body when it was getting hollowed out, there is virtually no simple way of replacing the head without damaging the rest of the decoy or your saw blade when you have to cut it off. A wooden dowel acts like a piece of plywood, adding strength to the neck when the grain of the dowel is epoxied in against the cross grain of the head and body. If it were to break, it can easily be cut off and replaced. Here I will use a 3/8" hardwood dowel, so I go one size larger (13/32") with the bit to drill a hole in the head. I start drilling in like this to prevent the bit from walking out of place. Once it starts, I can drill straight down through the head and neck into the body.

Once the epoxy is dry, I use a small hand saw to cut the excess off flush against the head.

I use a piece of tape to mark the depth I want to go into the body. Drilling all the way through the head, it only needs to run into the body about ½" to ¾" to do its work. I run the bit in and out of the hole to remove any excess cut wood and clean out the hole.

Before gluing in the dowel, I run it all the way into the hole and mark the side of the dowel with my pencil when it bottoms out. I mix up some more 5-minute epoxy and let some drizzle down into the hole and then coat the dowel with epoxy before inserting it into the hole. Air will get trapped in the hole, so I have to force the dowel in much like a syringe plunger. Air bubbles will come out, and at some point the excess epoxy will also flow out. I know my dowel is at the bottom of the hole when I see my mark. I then wipe up the excess epoxy and let it set up.

75

Turning to finishing off the tail, I use my pencil to round out both the top and underside of the tail. I use that big Scandi knife to cut in and flatten out the tail. I also use this big knife as a hand plane to thin the tail to the thickness I want it to be.

76

The next steps set off the Delaware River School diver from other styles. Using my pencil, I draw in my tail feathers and round out the tail.

77

Using my carving knife, I round out both sides of the tail, making sure they are symmetrical.

78

Using my basic carving knife, I cut in small V-cuts to define the tips of the tail feathers.

79

Using my straight-edged small detail knife, I cut straight in about ¹⁄₁₆" along the feather lines.

80

Going back to my standard carving knife, I carefully slice into the straight-in cut to define each feather. A little bit longer blade allows for more control and a shallower slice against the flat surface.

A bit of sanding will finish out the tail nicely. The underside of the tail is simply sanded flat.

Using a fine wood rasp, I finish out shaping the body, removing all the saw blade marks and spokeshave marks. John English and other Delaware River School carvers got their decoys fairly smooth. These are Dragon rasps from StewMac (stewmac.com). Remember to hit the crown of the head where the dowel is.

Once the rasp work is finished, I give the block a final sanding using 80-grit sandpaper. You can go finer if desired, but I like seeing some rasp and tool marks under the final paint in my decoys.

Many Delaware River carvers would go one step further with their decoys by carving in simple definition for the wing feathers. I use my pencil to draw the feather pattern I'll carve onto this block. By eye, I check the symmetry to make sure each side looks the same before committing my design to the knife.

Using a larger flat-edged utility-style knife, I cut straight in along my lines about ¹⁄₁₆" deep.

Once all of the straight-in cuts have been made, I follow up making a second angled cut that forms a shallow V into the first cut.

87

About there . . . all of the knife work is done.

88

It's time to brand this block. My brand is my signature. I get the iron super hot so it will brand deep into the wood.

PAINTING AND FINISHING

1

I seal the decoy using water-based spar urethane. The water will slightly raise the grain of the wood and also raise loose wood fibers. Once the urethane has dried, I lightly sand the block using 120-grit sandpaper.

2

Using my pencil, I draw in my paint pattern. It will be a very basic traditional bluebill: front third is black, middle is gray and white, and the back end is black.

3

Many early decoys on the East Coast used a spackling technique to suggest the vermiculation feather pattern found in many ducks. I use modern acrylic gesso for this. Back in the day, they used the lead white caulk to get this same effect. The consistency of the gesso straight from the container is perfect for this technique.

4

I paint a fairly thick coat of the gesso on the back where the duck's vermiculated back feathers are. I then place the flat bristles of the brush against the gesso and simply lift up. The tackiness of the gesso will create this neat, spackled texture. Let it dry overnight.

5

I'll use traditional flat decoy oil paints to paint this block. Flat Rust-Oleum is used for the white and Parker Decoy Paints are used for the other colors. The Parkers are very flat. The black is #5, the slate bluebill blue is #60, the earth brown is #41, and the yellow is #67.

6

I mix a medium dark gray using the white and black paints. This is painted completely over the white gesso spackling and allowed to thoroughly dry before doing any more painting.

7

Once the gray has dried, I use 120-grit sandpaper to lightly sand over the back. This removes the gray paint from the peaks of the spackling. Apply enough pressure to round off those peaks. Then dust off the decoy.

8

I paint the bill at this point using the Parker #60 slate bluebill blue. Parker paints may need a second coat as the paint is usually fairly thin, but they do dry quickly.

9

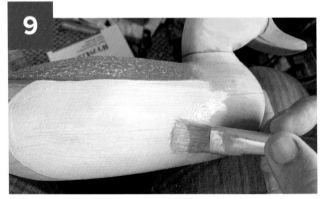

The Rust-Oleum is mixed thoroughly before being applied to the side pockets using a coarse bristle brush. This is an inexpensive craft brush. I use a bristle brush so it will leave brush marks in the paint. For the second coat, I will brush in a different direction and leave some gaps in the coat. Once the decoy is finished, the brushstrokes will show through, creating an aged appearance.

10

Once the white is dry to the touch, I paint the tail end of the decoy and also the bottom with the flat black. Again, I use a bristle craft brush so it will leave some stroke marks in the paint once it dries.

11

Once the black has dried, I paint the wing primaries over using the Parker #41 flat earth brown. I try to leave the black paint down in the V-channel. This will help define the wing feathers.

12

I paint the front of the decoy using the flat black. I'm careful applying the first coat so I have nice straight lines and avoid getting the black into other painted areas. I also take care to not get any flat black into the eyes. Once this first coat is fairly dry, I'll apply a second coat loosely over the first using the coarse bristle brush.

13

Using a small round brush and the flat black paint, I add the nail to the bill.

14

Using the Parker #67 yellow, I apply two coats of paint on each eye. Let this dry well.

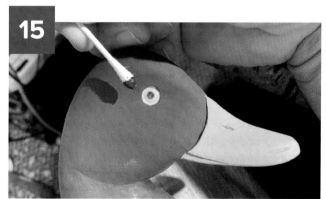

15

On a cotton swab, I twist the fibers tight around the head. I then dip the tip into my flat black paint. I carefully touch the swab to the eye, making the pupil.

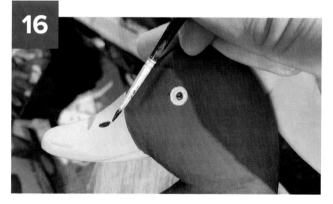

16

Using a small round detail brush, I fill in the nostril using the flat black paint.

Time to install the hardware on this block. I use old kitchen shears to cut a small leather tab for the front line tie. I also cut a piece of roofing lead that is approximately 1⁄16" thick by 3" long by 4½" wide. This width will be folded in half to make a double-thick piece that measures 3" by 2¼" wide.

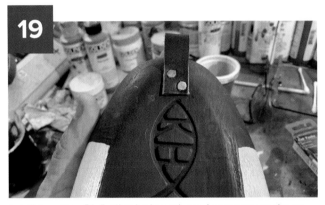

I drill two tiny 5⁄64" pilot holes where I want my tacks to go through the leather into the body. I place a drop of super glue in these holes and then drive my tacks into place. I drive the tacks in at opposing angles so they can't pull out.

When float-testing the block, I marked the lead's position with a pencil. I wanted the weight heavy to the rear to make the decoy ride better in the chop, as the traditional decoy makers did. Once the weight was flattened, I put a small layer of E6000 Glue on it and then put it in place on the decoy. I then lightly hammered it into the bottom shape of the decoy.

I double over the leather tab and place it on the front of the block. I use a drop of superglue to hold the loop together and another drop to hold the tab in place on the decoy.

Taking the lead pad weight out to my carving bench, I hammer the folded seam flat and then use the ball end of the hammer to flatten out all of the edges. Delaware River School decoys all used a flat pad weight for the ballast. This size flips the decoy quickly and should make the block float well in rougher water. A single layer of the lead this size did flip the decoy, but it flipped slowly and rode high in the water—not really what I want in a hunting decoy.

Once the lead is shaped to the body, I drill 5⁄64" pilot holes where I want my tacks.

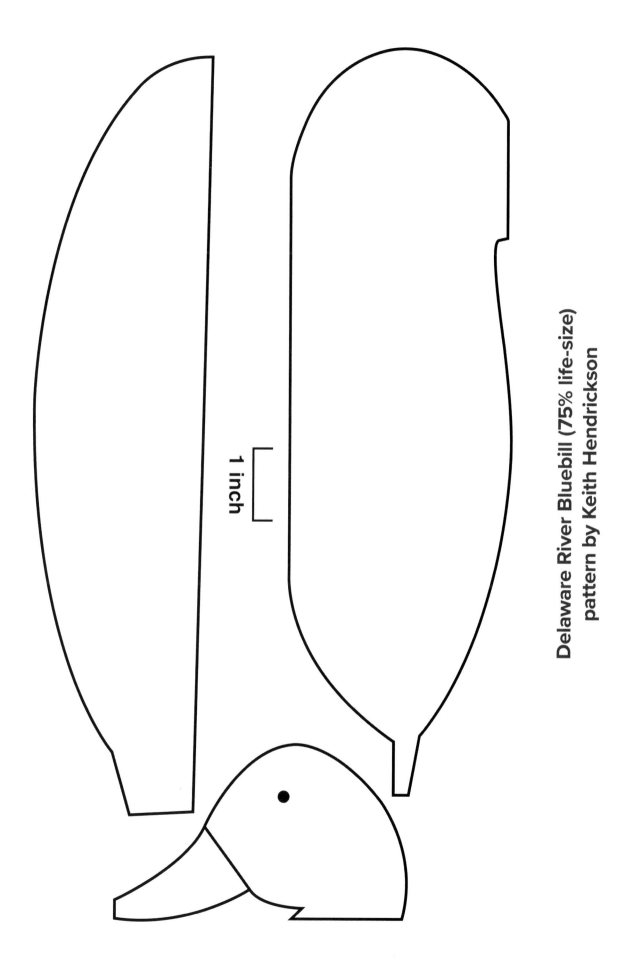

1 inch

**Delaware River Bluebill (75% life-size)
pattern by Keith Hendrickson**

CORE SOUND-STYLE RUDDY DUCK

North Carolina's Core Sound-style decoys can trace their influences to blocks carved on the Jersey and Maryland shores and on down the Chesapeake in the late 1800s and early 1900s. Many sportsmen from these areas brought their own stools down to the Carolinas when they hunted with the many famous gunning clubs along the Carolina shores. Local fishermen and boat builders also guided hunts at many of these clubs during the fall and winter migrations, so they saw these blocks and adapted many of the styles into their own carvings.

A true Core Sound bird could be made from many different materials, but it was often recycled from some other source. North Carolina's Outer Banks were notoriously treacherous for ships, and locals salvaged masts, decks, and hulls as well as rigging hardware from wrecks to make the area's somewhat primitive decoys. Carvers rarely had the money to acquire glass eyes for their birds, so they often gave their decoys carved or painted eyes. Many had no eyes at all. The makers also made ballast weight from flattened net weights, pieces of drive shafts, railroad spikes, or the heavy spikes used to secure the decks and hulls of the battered wrecks. It was also commonplace for the carvers to recycle other carvers' blocks that had drifted off or were discarded when heads broke off. This sometimes makes it difficult to identify the actual carvers.

Jerry Talton started carving decoys about two decades ago after he purchased a decoy for his brother's Christmas present. He was already a surfboard and skateboard maker and had many of the tools so he decided to try his hand at carving decoys. Living in the heart of the region where traditional Carolina carvers had chopped out their coastal stools, Jerry found carving resources everywhere. He gained inspiration from a copy of Jack Dudley's book, *Carteret Waterfowl Heritage*, and he obtained more information when he stopped by a small decoy shop in Betty, North Carolina, and met Gail Gerringer. Gail gave Jerry tips on wood selection and pattern drawing, but most importantly, she encouraged him to develop his own style. Curt Salter, one of the founding fathers of the Core Sound Decoy Carving Guild, encouraged Jerry to use traditional materials and hand tools to carve his birds.

As his style evolved, Jerry's work shifted to Core Sound-style decoys. Other influential carvers, including "Hurricane" Pete Peterson, J.P. Hand, Dr. Chuck May, and Walter "Brother" Gaskill, pushed Jerry to make truly traditional decoys instead of decoys that looked traditional. Being a true perfectionist, Jerry set out to do the absolute best at whatever he is doing.

Jerry's ruddy pattern is a beautiful representation of a classic Core Sound-style decoy from the days of market gunning. It is fairly simple to carve and uses traditional juniper or white cedar as the wood. These blocks were normally chopped out using a hatchet and carving knife. A few nails attached the heads and the painting was minimal, usually using what was left in the boat shed.

TOOLS

- Carving hatchet
- Tack hammer
- Straight-edged and curve-edged carving knives
- Bent blade carving knife
- Scorp
- Spoon plane
- Spokeshave
- Sculptor's adze
- Round hand gouges
- Bar clamps
- Heavy, large sanding block and coarse sandpaper
- Assorted paintbrushes
- $3/8$" Forstner bit
- $1/8$" long drill bit
- 1" fishtail skew
- Hand drill
- Branding iron and heat source

MATERIALS

- Rusted $1\frac{1}{2}$" nails (Tremontnail.com CLR4)
- $3\frac{1}{2}$" stainless self-tapping screw
- Titebond III
- White quick-drying Gorilla Glue
- Tapered wooden plugs $7/16$"

Jerry starts his bird with a typical cutout done on the band saw. He uses two pieces for a lighter block, hollowing the two halves before gluing them together. He made this particular decoy body from two pieces of juniper. He used a pair of screws to hold the pieces together while cutting on the band saw, paying attention to the grain of the wood to ensure the hatchet cuts the wood instead of splitting it. Try to keep the center of the tree grain toward the center of the decoy to avoid splits. Note that the chine line on this pattern matches the line the two halves will form.

Remove the screws separating the two halves and then mark your cut points for hollowing the bird with a pencil. Make notes on the shallower areas at the tail and head. You won't want to go too deeply in these areas to avoid cutting through the body when you actually carve the block.

Sitting on a traditional New Jersey-style carver's bench, Jerry uses a sculptor's adze to make his initial cuts into the center of each half. If you are not comfortable using hatchet type tools, you can also do this with large gouges or a carving scorp.

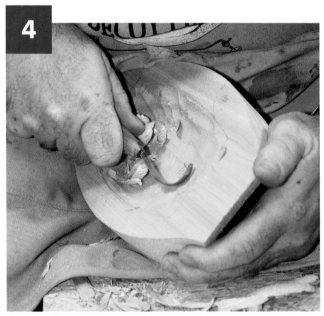

After making the initial deep cuts, Jerry removes most of the wood with a gouge, switching over to a bent knife to clean things up.

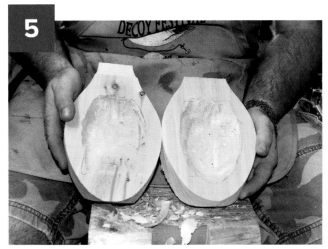

5

This is how the two halves should look once you have finished hollowing.

7

While the glue is drying, start the head. Kiln-dried wood is best here. On your cutout, draw in the bill line on each side of the head. Extend this line across the top and bottom of the head.

8

While holding your pencil, use your middle finger as a guide against the wood to mark a line on both sides of the head to mark your bill width.

6

Jerry glues the two halves together using the quick-drying white Gorilla Glue. He wets one side per gluing instructions, and then runs a double ring of glue around one of the halves. He places the halves together and, using the top flat cutout, matches them up and clamps them together to allow the glue to dry thoroughly.

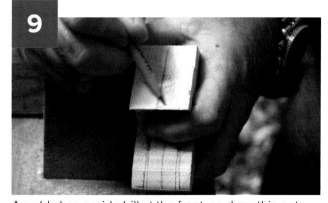

9

A ruddy has a wide bill at the front, so draw this onto the bottom of the bill, flaring it out to the front about ⅛" on each side. Then draw in your centerline all the way around the head. At the base of the neck, draw in your neck circle and round out the corners.

10

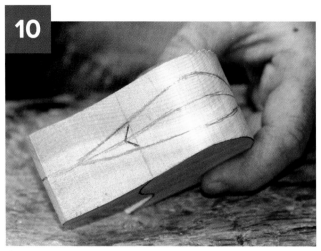

On the top side of the head, draw in the V-notch of the bill, indicating the top of the bill width (about ⅜"), the flattened V portion of the bill, and the top of the crown (¾" wide).

12

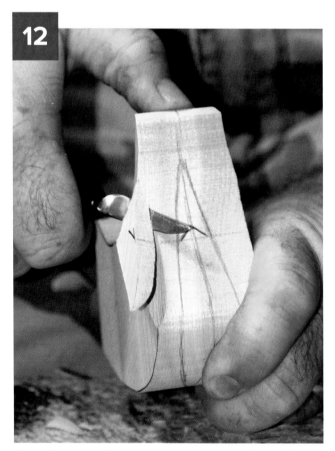

From the top of the head, start carving in the front taper into the bill and begin shaping the bill. Work on both sides of the head at the same time, cutting into your guidelines to insure you get things symmetrical without carving in too far. Avoid carving too far into the front of the face, too.

11

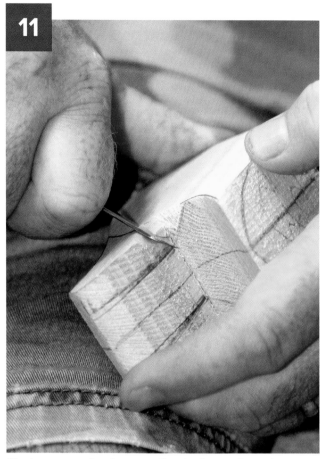

Start your carving by rounding in the neck on the underside of the head. Make a good ½" deep cut straight into the head right at the line at the base of the bill. Then remove the wood on each side of this cut. Do this on both sides of the bill and then extend the front portion of the cuts forward along the bill width lines.

13

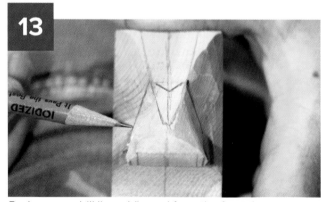

Redraw your bill lines. Viewed from the front these lines should be nice and straight. If you see them curve outward anywhere, this indicates an area where you need to do more carving. Make sure the curves are symmetrical when you look down on the top of the head.

14

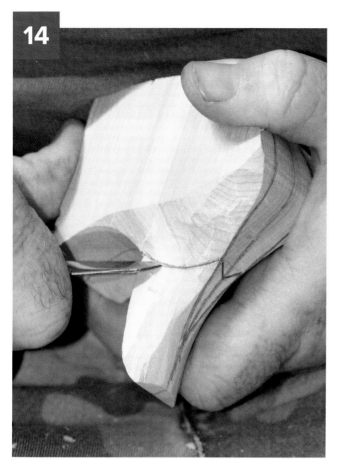

Now slice in the bill margins. Starting at the top of the bill, slice from the bill into the head, angling to the back slightly. Do this on both sides.

16

Now slice in from the cheek into your initial cut to remove the wood from the cheek, defining the bill. Then round out the neck on both sides at the front of the throat.

15

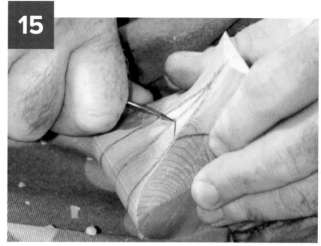

Cut straight in for the V-notch and then angle down into your cut from the top of the head.

17

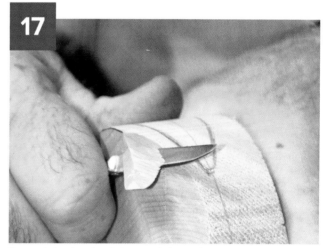

Round the back of the neck from the base of the neck on up to the crown of the head. Round and shape the tip of the bill, leaving enough thickness to keep the bill strong. Then check the head from top, bottom, and both sides to ensure everything is symmetrical.

18

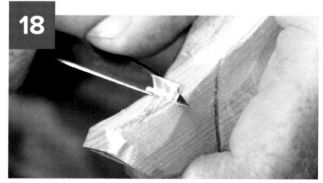

Flatten the top of the bill and make sure there are no saw marks showing from your initial cutout.

19

Carve in the neck slightly to define the cheek and then sand the entire head. You don't have to get it completely smooth and can even leave a few coarse sand marks here and there.

21

Now that the glue has dried, remove your clamps from the body. If you used screws to hold the body together while doing the initial cutout, it is time to fill these holes. Jerry drills out the screw holes with a ⅜" Forstner bit and then fills them with tapered wooden plugs, matching the direction of the grain in the plug with the grain in the body. Apply a small amount of Titebond III to the holes, tap in the plugs, then use a flat chisel or skew to cut the plug off flush with the bottom of the block.

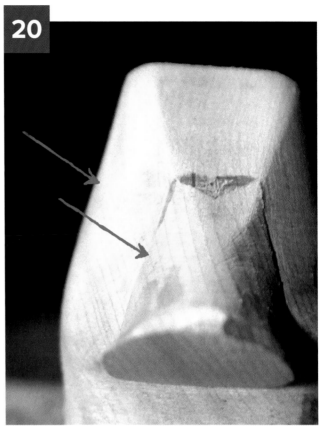

20

Looking at the head from the front, a typical Core Sound-style bird will be fairly flat from the cheek to the crown of the head and the angle of the bill will match the angle of the front profile of the head.

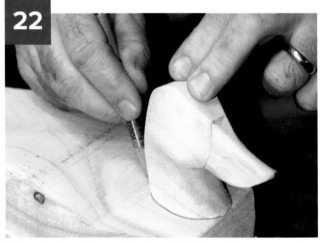

22

Place the head onto the head shelf and draw around it to indicate the head placement. You can also draw in an arrow pointing in the direction the head will be turned if you decide to turn it.

23

Draw in your centerline all the way around the bird. Also draw in lines indicating the "ice scoop," the cut that allows water to flow from the back on down around the neck. Add marks for the peak on the shoulders, and a mark showing the high point on the back.

24

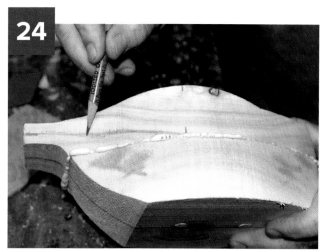

Transfer the high point on the back to the side and mark it. Continue the line down to the center of the chine where the halves are glued together and make another mark. Now draw a line from the center of the tail down to this center point. This will be the back chine on the bird. The front chine is the cut. Do the same on the other side.

25

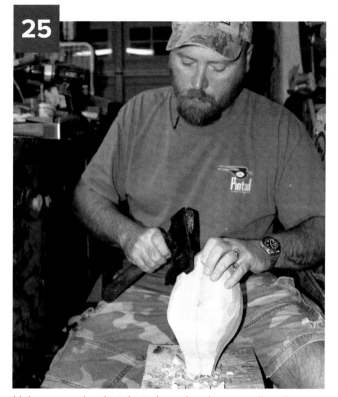

Using a carving hatchet, Jerry begins rounding the bottom front of the bird. He rotates and positions the bird so he can maintain the same chopping motion at the same angle. The hatchet moves along the same plane at all times. Carve the bird in quarters. Do the bottom front first as one quarter. Switch to the back end as the second quarter. Round up from the bottom to the chines on the sides. Then touch up the bottom by rounding the bottom sides to make the front lines and curves flow to the back.

26

Switch to the top of the bird. Work on rounding down both sides towards the tail, making sure you don't cut too far over your guidelines. Then round forward, making sure you leave the high areas at the front of each shoulder.

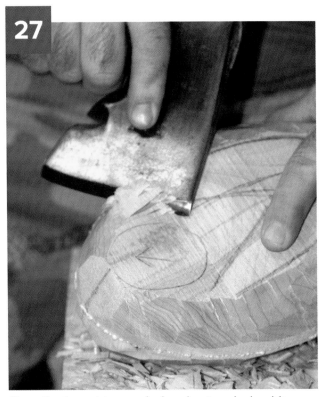

27

Once the breast is round, chop in at each shoulder from the back forward to set your shoulder depth. Note the angle of the cut runs from the cape forward to the breast.

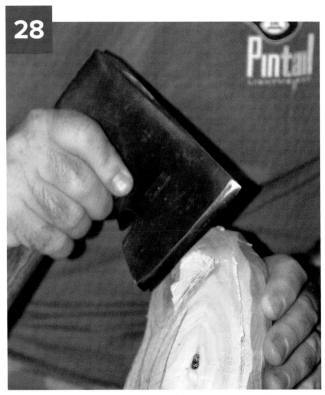

28

Flip the bird around and carefully chop in against the grain up to your previous shoulder cuts to remove the wood in front of the shoulders.

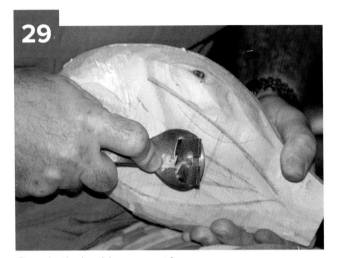

29

Once both shoulders are cut in, use a scorp or a spoon plane to cut the ice scoop from the cape down and in from the middle of the back to the head shelf.

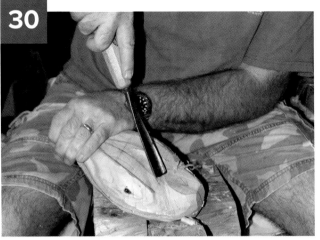

30

With a large round gouge, finish cutting from the ice scoop on down to the breast, between the shoulder and the head shelf. This helps form the transition from the neck of the bird into the body.

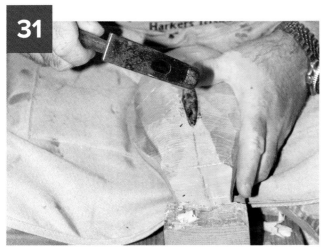

At this point, all the chopping is done. Using a spokeshave, knife, and flat fishtail skew, Jerry refines the body shape and symmetry. On the bottom of the bird, he works up a flat spot to locate the small pad weight. Placing the weight into position at the end of the keel line, he uses a hammer to tap and shape the weight to match the curve of the bottom of the bird. Outline the weight location with a pencil onto the bottom.

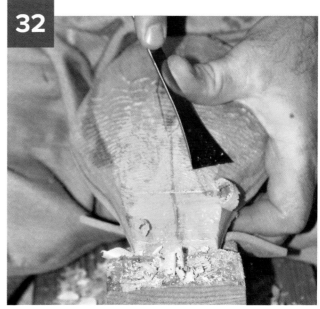

Jerry uses a flat fishtail skew to carve and shape the tail on both sides. A curve blade knife is also useful working in the transition area of the tail and body. Check the bottom and top for symmetry and make any needed adjustments with a knife or spokeshave.

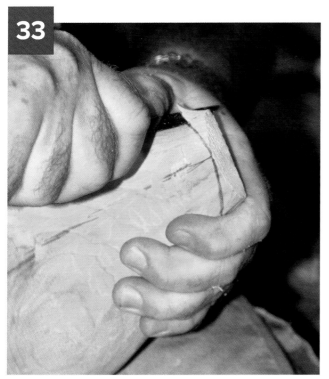

Use your pencil to draw in the tail's shape. Round the tail and thin it to the desired thickness with a knife.

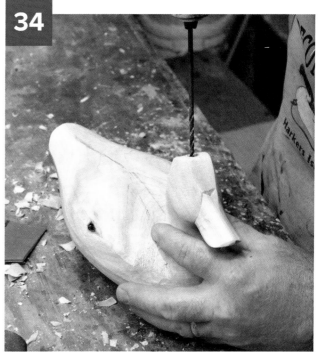

A 3½" stainless self-tapping screw, running down through the center of the neck, will attach the head to the body. Use a ⅜" Forstner bit and sink a hole about ⅜ of an inch deep into the back of the head. Position this hole where it will run through the center of the neck. Then use a long ⅛" drill bit and drill a pilot hole the rest of the way through the head for the main head screw.

35

Put some Titebond III on the head shelf and attach the head, running the self-tapping 3½" stainless screw through the pilot hole you drilled through the head. Run it snugly into the body.

36

Place some glue into the top of the screw hole and plug the hole with a tapered wooden plug. Trim the plug to match the shape of the head and sand the plug smooth.

37

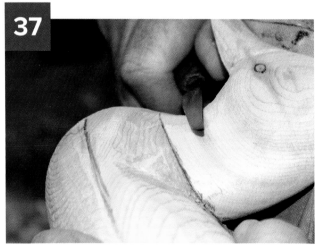

Using your knife, carve in a nice neck transition from the head into the body. Instead of sandpaper, Jerry uses a scrape at this point to knock off all of the rough spots. He leaves most of the tool marks on the body.

38

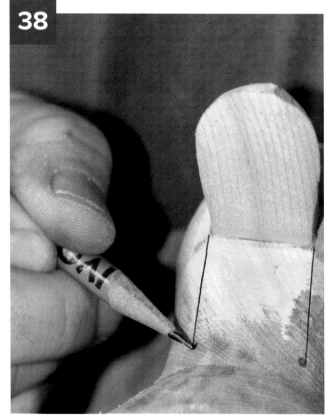

At the front of the head, draw in two lines straight down from the edges of the bill. Mark points where you will drill pilot holes angled slightly back into the body.

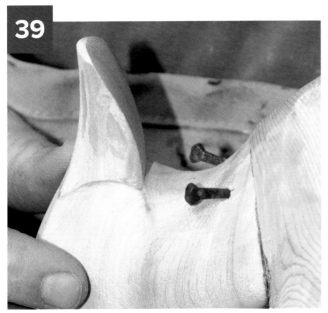

39

With the ⅛" bit, drill your pilot holes through the neck and on into the body about ½" deep. Place a rusty tack nail into each hole and using a punch, tap in the nails and counter-sink them a bit.

40

Your bird is now ready to finish and antique.

PAINTING AND FINISHING

Something just seems to draw us to old, rough, beat-up decoys. Maybe we like to imagine the stories the old blocks would tell if they could talk. They've been hunted over, thrown under skiffs as soon as the season went out, and at some point probably repainted. Paint layer covered paint layer as the years passed. Some of the old blocks received a few accidental drips of boat paint, depending on where they landed under that skiff during the off season. It took decades for time to add its natural patina to true antique birds.

The paint technique of true Core Sound-style decoys is as simple as it gets. The decoy makers applied block-style paint to the birds with whatever paint was available in the boathouse. Usually basic black, white, and brown oils made up the palette. Jerry uses a traditional paint style for this ruddy duck. His antiquing method takes about two weeks to finish so he often works on several birds at a time. He starts out by staining the carved block and follows that by applying a thinned paint layer as a primer. After allowing for drying time, Jerry moves rapidly after adding the final paint layer and then using some interesting but workable methods to partially remove it. So let's get started and add a few decades to this newly carved block.

MATERIALS

- Quart can of flat white Rust-Oleum
- 3 37 ml tubes of raw umber oil paint
- 1 tube of French ultramarine oil paint
- Pint can of Ronan raw umber oil paint
- Mineral spirits and turpentine
- Sawdust

- Paper bags
- Rusted staple and ring or leather tab
- Small pad weight for ballast
- Slurry stain of water, tobacco, and coffee grounds
- Citristrip paint-and-varnish removing gel

Antiquing the bird actually takes the better part of two weeks to complete. Jerry starts off with a slurry stain made of water, dried tobacco leaves, and old coffee grounds. He simply paints the entire bird with this stain solution. Notice how areas with raw tool marks better absorb the stain while sanded areas absorb it differently. Once you're done, set the bird aside and let it dry for a day or two.

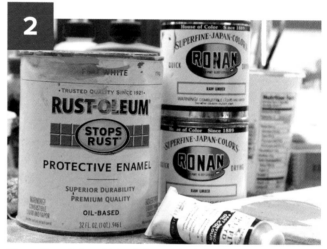

Once the stained block has dried, Jerry applies an initial layer of thinned oil paint. The antique white Jerry uses for all of his paints comes from a quart can of Rust-Oleum flat white, oil-based enamel mixed well with two 37 ml tubes of raw umber oil paints. He'll also use a pint can of Ronan flat raw umber and a tube of French ultramarine blue.

Make some paint thinner with a 50/50 mineral spirits and turpentine. Using the Ronan raw umber, thin down the paint to the point where it's almost a stain. Paint half the body, and then blot it down with a clean rag. Do the same to the other side. By doing only one half at a time, you prevent the paint from drying too much before blotting. Blotting the paint instead of wiping it down creates texture that will help you build up layers of what will look like old paint in later steps.

Paint the rest of the head with the thinned raw umber. Blot off when you are done.

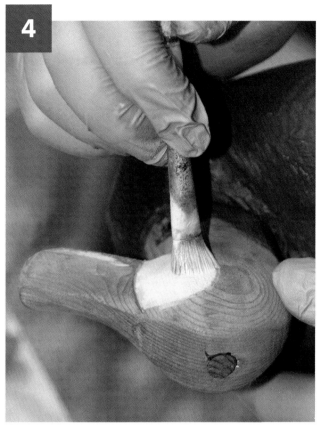

Now thin down some of the antiqued white and paint in the cheek patches, working a bit from one side, then the other. Make sure both sides are the same size and in the same location, checking from the front and top of the head. Blot the white down with a cloth.

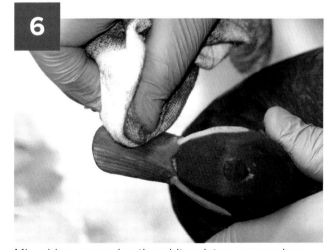

Mix a blue-gray using the white mixture, raw umber, and French ultramarine. Thin it down to the the consistency of a thick stain and paint the bill. Blot off excess paint. Lay the bird aside and let it dry for four days.

7

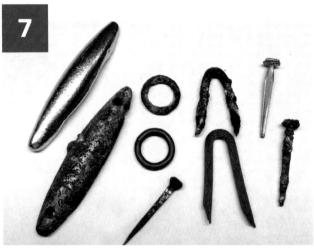

Once the paint-stained bird has dried, it is time to add hardware. Jerry uses an old metal-cast mold for elongated fishing weights to pour his ballast weights for the decoy's bottom. Leaving the two-part mold open, he pours the molten lead into the open halves of the weight to make a pair of pad weights instead of a single fishing weight. Old-style decoy makers typically used these pad weights on many blocks. Jerry puts all the hardware, including the poured weights, outside in the weather so they will rust and corrode. Drill a hole through the weight on both ends so you can pass a nail through it. You will need two rusted nails to secure the weight to the body. You will also need a rounded steel staple and steel ring (also rusted).

9

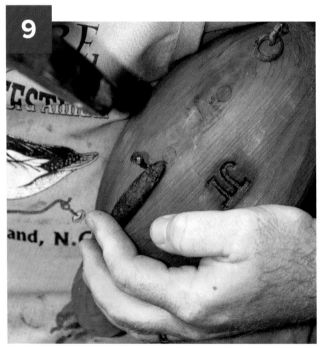

Use the rusted nails to attach the weight to the bottom tail end of the bird.

8

Position the staple and ring and mark hole locations. Drill small pilot holes into the bird to keep the tack from splitting the wood. Use a tack hammer to drive the staple partially into the decoy, allowing the ring to swing freely. Many traditional carvers used a loop of leather or canvas instead of a tack and ring to serve as their line tie.

10

Time for the final paint layer. Using full-strength paint, mix the white, umber, and ultramarine combination to make the blue-gray for the bill. Paint this on thickly, so it's nearly ready to run.

11

For the white cheek patch, mix the antique white with a touch of raw umber and a dash of powdered pumice. You want this mix to be chunky and streaky. Apply it on both sides as thickly as you can get them without the paint running down the side of the cheek.

12

Paint the rest of the head with Ronan's raw umber. Keep the paint thick.

13

Moisten a clean brush with thinner, blot it off, and run it completely around the white cheek patch without lifting the brush. When you get to the other end of the patch, flip the brush to the clean side and run it back the other direction. Start at the top for the first pass and then at the bottom for the second pass. Doing this will keep the white portion of the brush on the white cheek for both runs. This will blend the umber head into the white cheek.

14

Jerry cups the decoy in his hand and paints the entire back with thick Ronan raw umber.

15

Holding the line tie ring, paint the bottom of the bird with raw umber.

16

Take the decoy outside while the paint is still very wet and hose off the entire bird with water spray. This beats down the paint and will also help flatten it a bit. It will also bubble up under some of the wet paint to weaken the paint layer in places, all part of the antiquing process.

17

Set the decoy on a drying rack or hang it from the ring to partially dry off for 45 minutes.

18

After 45 minutes there will still be a few water drops on the decoy but that is fine. Take the bird back out to the hose. Using a wide bristle brush and paint the entire bird with Citristrip paint-and-varnish stripping gel. As soon as you've covered the bird, spray it with the hose. The water immediately neutralizes the stripper. Blot the bird dry with a clean cloth and then set it aside to dry and cure for 4 days.

19

Once the decoy has cured, beat down any sharp edges along the top of the head, bill, and tail and here and there along the back, using a piece of 2 x 4 wrapped with coarse sandpaper. This distresses the paint and wood in places. Just hit a few places...don't overdo it.

20

Make a very thin solution of weak tube raw umber and turpentine. Use your gloved hand to rub this solution all over the bird, including the hardware. Rub well into the knocked surfaces and massage it into the wood, paint, and hardware.

21

When the bird is half tacky, get sawdust on your hand and rub it all over the bird. This absorbs the turpentine. It also sticks into the cracks and brand; adding to the antiqued look.

22

While the bird is still a bit wet, place a small paper bag over your hand and start rubbing and polishing. Rub like crazy. This will create and accelerate the decoy's patina.

23

Once the bird has dried for several days, you can once again polish it with the brown paper bag. More shine will develop over time.

24

Jerry finishes his new antiques by flicking a bit of bright colored paint across the back of the bird. Hunters often stored their stools in boat sheds where they might drip anti-fowling hull paint on them when maintaining their boats in the off season.

25

A ruddy, painted and antiqued.

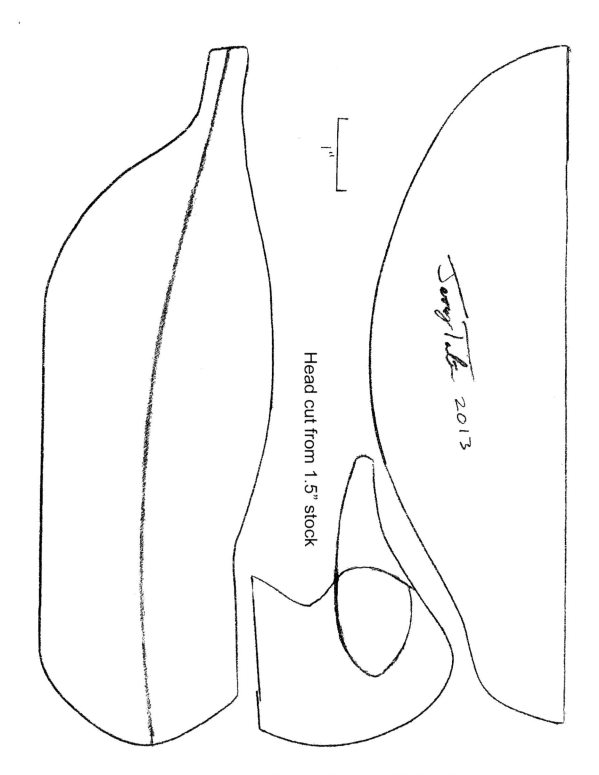

Head cut from 1.5" stock

1"

Jerry Talton 2013

Core Sound-Style Ruddy Duck (75% life-size)

pattern by Jerry Talton

DELTA MARSH CANVASBACK

I've always been interested in older-looking decoys. I've never been able to afford to collect them, so knowing the specifics to some of those old classics has allowed me to carve my rendition of the blocks and actually hunt over them in my own spread. The first carver that came to mind when I started working on this project does a similar thing. Pat Gregory is an Illinois carver that carves and hunts over many different historic northern styles of decoys. He carves Illinois River blocks, Michigan feather-stamped blocks, and also a Canadian style that looks like no others. Pat is the great grandson of famed Illinois River carver George "Homerun" Barto, of Tiskelwa, Illinois. He is a waterfowling purist in that he carves with traditional tools, uses traditional classic boats, and hunts over hand-carved decoys. Pat learned to carve from mentor Art Behemetuik, who was a student of Barto. He began carving in 1984 and carves 100 to 200 decoys a year.

I first took note of Pat's carvings a few years ago when he posted some folkish looking canvasbacks on his Facebook page. The interesting primitive blocks were thankfully accompanied with some fascinating history on the decoys. The blocks were carved by Pat and his images also included authentic decoys carved by one of the original carvers of the style known as the Delta Marsh decoy. This carver, Duncan Ducharme (1912-1972), carved the decoys by the thousands along with working as a hunting guide on the marsh for James Ford Bell and other prominent duck hunters/clubs in the region.

Pat's photos and brief history lesson were neat but became much more relevant after the passing of one of my family's dogs, a somewhat shaggy, mottled-brown German wirehaired pointer. This pooch belonged to my daughter and loved the marsh. She was a bit hardheaded and was interestingly different: her own character. She deserved an old, brown, mottled decoy as her ash urn that was different. I began hunting information on the decoy whose image was etched in the back of my mind, and it didn't take long to get up with Pat to find out more information on the block that one could say defines Canada's Delta Marsh.

Before I dive into carving this block, one needs to understand the history behind the stylish bird and know that there is one carver, Duncan Ducharme, who is most relevant for the style, but he was backed by a prominent businessman, his family, and an entire community in developing the Delta Marsh canvasback.

Ducharme carved blocks. (All photos on this page by Fred Greenslade, Delta Waterfowl.)

Hen with a Gaylord rig metal keel.

Pat Gregory.

Duncan Ducharme. (Photo by Joe and Donna Tonelli via the Ducharme family.)

An original Duncan Ducharme block out of the Bell rig. (Photo by Donna Tonelli.)

The Bell family, specifically James Ford Bell (the founder of General Mills) enjoyed waterfowling for canvasback. His favorite home gunning spot was Heron Lake, located in the southwestern part of Minnesota. Heron was a fall staging lake for canvasback and was full of sago pondweed, a favorite food for waterfowl. But the food source was on a tragic decline in the lake due to farming runoff and carp infestation, so Bell decided to try and find a new area to hunt in. It was just after World War I when Bell settled on an area known as the Delta Marsh located on the southern end of Lake Manitoba. Bell established a hunt camp on the property he bought, and built a new lodge to base hunts out of.

Looking at the shape of the breast on this hen canvasback, one can get an idea where the folkish body shape came from on these decoys.

About the time the Delta hunt camp was getting started, Edward Ward heard about the possibilities of managing the property. He made his way to the farm by foot and began working for Bell, managing the grounds, lodge, and a duck hatchery, part of the Delta Waterfowl Research Center Bell also started. Edward raised his family, three sons and five daughters, on the property, and all of the boys worked there to some degree. As the first duck season at the new camp approached, Bell had part of his Heron Lake canvasback rig sent up.

This original Heron Lake rig was most likely carved by Abe Nelson (1884-1972). Bell gave one of the original Heron Lake birds to Little Joe Ducharme and his brother Dan to start carving the decoys in mass numbers. Little Joe was an artist and craftsman and worked to improve the Heron Lake decoy's serviceability to fit the needs of the Delta Marsh, but his productivity fell short of Bell's patience and expectations. To speed up production, Bell decided to have the initial decoys mass produced on a duplicating jig back at one of the mills in Minneapolis. Once the first shipment of decoys was finished and shipped, the Canadian customs considered them works of art and hit Bell with a high import tax, so Bell then decided to ship the decoys in pieces, unfinished, and let Ward deal with finishing the decoys.

Ward distributed the roughed-out blocks to the Ducharmes and several other local guides. The Ducharmes (the club's guides) and other locals quickly formed a cottage industry to finish and paint the blocks. The family, headed by Little Joe, Dan, and Joe's son Duncan, eventually took over all of the decoy manufacturing. Duncan made the canvasback decoys by the thousands and was by far the most prolific carver of the Delta Marsh-styled canvasback. He carved many of the decoys out of discarded telegraph poles and fence posts, chopping them out with a hatchet and finishing them with a hand rasp. He produced the decoys not only for Bell, but also the many other clubs around and near the marsh, including the Sports Afield Camp built by Jimmy Robinson, and the Waterhen Lodge built by the Gaylord family.

It is believed that as many as 100 different local craftsmen helped produce the now stylized decoy by the thousands for many of the clubs around Delta Marsh. Some carvers produced heads, some bodies, some rasped out and sanded the blocks, and others, like the Ward family, painted the blocks. The Ward boys along with their brother-in-law, Al Hochbaum (noted waterfowl biologist that worked at the research center), were all artistic and are credited for carving and painting many of the Delta-styled canvasbacks, along

Beautiful drake block carved by Pat Gregory.

Top view showing the teardrop shape of the decoys. Side view showing the blunt angled ends. Bottom view showing the deep wooden keel and strip weight. James Ford Bell brand. (All photos on this page by Pat Gregory.)

with many other fine decoys and flat art. Torry was quite the carver, painter, and even collector. Peter Ward is credited for painting many different rigs and although his paint pattern looked somewhat primitive in hand, the blotches of paint blended perfectly on the water to make the decoy appear to be real. (It is Peter's paint pattern on his hen decoys that reminded me of the coloration on my dog.)

Duncan Ducharme carved the bodies of his Delta Marsh Canvasbacks out of solid white cedar and used white pine for the heads. Many of them had a steep angled pointed breast and rump where others were rounded on the breast and rump. The decoy almost appeared to have been carved backwards for some reason or another and this teardrop shape was brought up from the original Heron Lake rig, although these birds were a bit more rounded or egg-shaped looking at the bottom profile. Some called the shape "clunky" or "folky," but this day and age, I would call them "stealthy" looking. The necks on the birds were tall and sloping with a solid reinforcing dowel running down from the top of the head on into the body. The heads on most of the birds were nearly centered on the body and had no eyes, but some of them did have tack eyes. Some heads had basic "industrial" carving intended for hunting with a strong bill and neck, while others had what some called a "horse" head with finer bill carving and a rounder cheeky head shape.

Pat Gregory was kind enough to share the more traditional pattern that Duncan Ducharme used, pulling it directly from one of Ducharme's decoys in Pat's collection. It is a fairly small block, measuring only 12" long by 6" wide. For this carving demonstration, I drafted my apprentice, Jonathan Mauldin, to carve a block from Pat's pattern so I could take the accompanying photographs.

Lay out the pattern on your block of wood. At the least, you will need a piece measuring 12" x 6" x 4" thick. Lay out the head pattern on a separate piece of wood that is 2" thick.

Using your band saw, cut your body out as we have done in previous demonstrations.

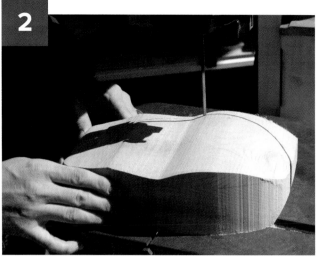

Cut the head out, ensuring the grain in the wood runs the same direction straight down the bill.

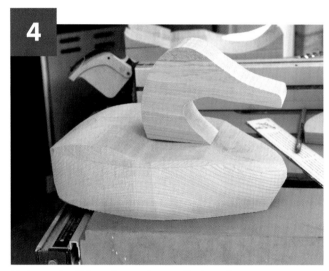

Using a flexible ruler and pencil, draw in your centerlines down the middle of the head and also the body. Mark in the approximate location of where the head will come into the body.

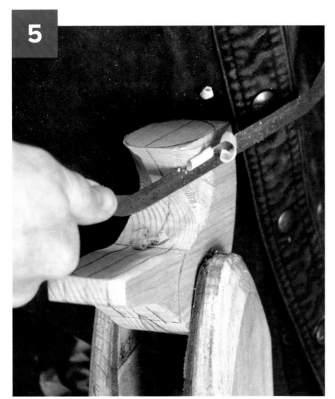

5

Begin rounding out the head, removing excess wood. Round out the neck, being careful not to chip out wood around the base of the neck.

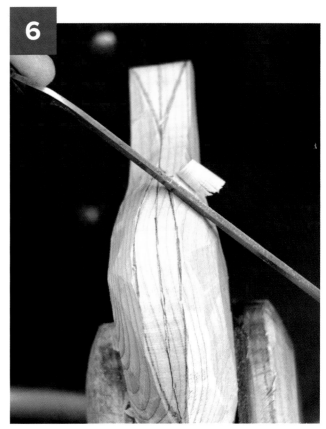

6

Continuing carving the head working into the bill. Typically these heads were narrow; less than 2" thick and carving was very basic.

7

Once the bulk of the wood has been removed, switch to a knife and refine your carving to remove any flat spots on the cheeks. The crown of the head can be flat or rounded.

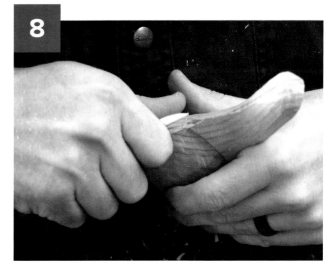

8

Cut in the margins of the bill. Make a first cut straight in and a second cut angled into the first from the feather side of the head. This makes it easy to paint the bill cleanly.

9

Begin rounding out the body. If you don't hatchet carve, you can use a drawknife to remove the excess wood. This is where many of the original decoys varied. Some had totally flat bottoms and some were rounded up from the bottom. Some were flat in the mid-section and rounded on the ends.

10

Round up to the back removing all of the bulk wood. Be careful not to get too close to the head/neck shelf where the head will get mounted later.

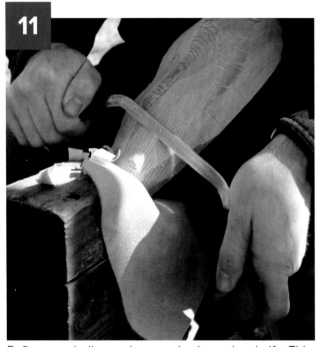

11

Refine your bulk wood removal using a drawknife. This should be the point where you can really see the block taking shape.

12

Finish refining the shape using a spokeshave. Carefully work your way up to the head shelf. Place the head on occasionally to carve in a nice, angled transition from the breast up into the neck.

13

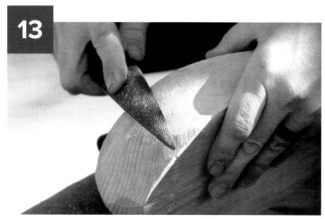

Duncan Ducharme finished shaping the decoy using a rasp. He did little to no sanding after this point to keep a rough texture on his working birds. This really did dull the decoy and kept it from shining too much on the water.

14

Glue the head on and, using the rasp, smooth the angle from the front of the neck into the body.

15

Using a $^{25}/_{64}$" drill bit, drill a hole from the top of the head on into the body. Start the bit at an angle 90 degrees to the slope in the head and then once the bit has started cutting, you can straighten it up to drill straight down through the neck. This will prevent the bit from walking down the slope of the neck.

16

Using epoxy or Gorilla Glue, glue in a hardwood dowel. Trim and rasp the dowel once the glue has dried.

17

Nails through the neck are optional. At this point the carving is complete. Sand the bird some if desired and then seal and prime the wood using a good oil-based primer.

18

Paint is very simple: block painted wild blotches suggesting feather detail. If you are going to hunt over your decoy, I suggest using an oil-based paint like Ronan, flat Rust-Oleum, or Parker Decoy Paints. If you use latex paints, seal the paint using a flat varnish coat of some sort like Krylon.

19

Attach your wooden keel. The actual Delta Marsh canvasbacks used a deep keel with a strap weight nailed to the bottom of the keel. Duncan made a rig for the Gaylord family that used a neat metal keel they manufactured at the Ingersol Rand plant that was simply nailed onto the bottom of the decoys.

20

Once the keel is attached, you can finish the bottom of the decoy using paint, spar varnish/urethane, or epoxy.

21

Delta Marsh Gracey ash urn.

Delta Marsh Canvasback
pattern by Pat Gregory

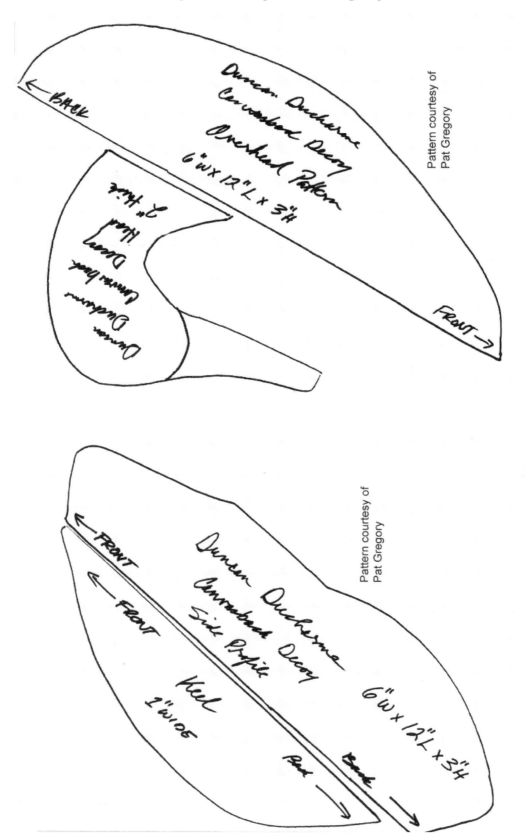

Duncan Ducharme
Canvasback Decoy
Overhead Pattern
6"W x 12"L x 3"H

Duncan Ducharme
Canvas back
Decoy Head
2" thick

BACK

FRONT

Pattern courtesy of
Pat Gregory

Duncan Ducharme
Canvasback Decoy
Side Profile
6"W x 12"L x 3"H

FRONT

FRONT

Keel
1"wide

Back

Back

Pattern courtesy of
Pat Gregory

BARNEGAT BAY BLACK DUCK

Scientists estimate that 70% of the black ducks that migrate along the Atlantic flyway winter in New Jersey. If you look at a coastal map of the state, you can see why. New Jersey has thousands of small tidal creeks that drain the marshes and make up what is called the salt meadows. The area provides a perfect habitat for wintering waterfowl, especially black ducks. These meadows line the eastern side of the state, while the western side has the Delaware Bay and River. With so much coastal waterfowl habitat, it's no wonder New Jersey has a rich decoy history.

I contacted Jamie (JP) Hand, a New Jersey native and historian who has been carving traditional decoys for more than 50 years. I met him at a carving workshop where he was teaching how to carve a traditional hollow-bodied New Jersey black duck. Jamie is from Cape May County and learned to carve from Hurley Conklin (Manahawkin, New Jersey, 1913-1993) and Harry V. Shourds II (1930-2017). He explained that two basic carving styles came out of New Jersey and that they coincide with the state's two coastal regions: the east coast salt meadows, and the west coast Delaware Bay/River. The Delaware River School decoys often have nicely carved, raised wingtips and use a flat lead pad on the bottom of the decoy for ballast. This chapter will cover a well-known decoy pattern that originated in the east coast and is often called the Barnegat Bay School. Because this covers a much larger area than just Barnegat Bay, many refer to the style simply as the Jersey Shore School.

I didn't think I would be revisiting the black duck so soon, but after I learned that a great uncle of mine had been a well-known decoy carver from Northfield, New Jersey, I wanted to dig deeper into the history with a 100-year-old puddle duck pattern. My curiosity was sparked by an old black duck I managed to get from George Strunk that had been carved by Joseph Eugene (Gene) Hendrickson (1899-1971). It was in rough but original shape. Once I got my hands on the decoy, I found the body shape was a good bit different than the Jersey Shore School black duck decoys we carved in Jamie's class. It had a steep hump on its back and the bottom ballast weight was cut into the bottom of the old block.

One of the early decoy characteristics shared by H.V. Shourds, Mark Kears, and Gene Hendrickson was the humped, deep-drop tail.

My initial research on the old block showed that Gene carved close to the same pattern as his neighbor and close friend, Mark Kears (1888-1972). The elder Kears' carving was influenced by other nearby carvers: Harry V. Shourds and Mark English. Shourds (and later his son and grandson) carved many black ducks that showed the same tall, humped style called a deep-drop tail, so most likely the pattern was a family pattern. Decoy makers back then often shared patterns, so it would not be unusual for Kears to pass his pattern along to Hendrickson. Even though the carvers used the same pattern, they had unique carving styles, so we can identify their work. Hendrickson began carving around 1914 and hunted the narrow creeks in the marsh meadows, so his decoys during this period were relatively small. The rumps were tall, and the heads were full with fairly fat cheeks. The bill margins, where the bill meets the head, were carved in and well defined, as were the bill and nostril carvings. As time passed, the deep-drop tail pattern became less pronounced, and the overall size grew a bit as the demand for larger decoys grew. Gene also moved from hunting the small creeks to the larger bays, where a larger decoy drew more birds.

Gene Hendrickson's original decoy is at top. My carving replicates his style, but I took some liberties with the painting.

One of the most notable characteristics of the Barnegat-Jersey Shore School is the carved inlet for the ballast weight. The maker would use a ¾" flat wood chisel to cut in a rectangular inlet around 3 inches long into the bottom of the hollowed decoy and then fill the inlet with molten lead. According to Harry V. Shourds II (the grandson), black ducks need around five ounces of lead to make them self-right and ride correctly. Jamie Hand told me the more skilled carvers would undercut the ends of the inlet much like a dovetail to prevent the lead from working loose over time. Some carvers, like Hurley Conklin, used a round wood bit to bore in the ends of the inlet and then finished out the depth and length with the chisel. To contain the lead, they would hammer in two nails set at angles and leave the heads exposed in the inlet. Once the lead was poured in, it would set with the nails inside, preventing the lead from loosening up. Hendrickson used the dovetail method on his decoys.

Gene Hendrickson used small metal upholstery tacks for the eyes. Finish nails secured the heads, and longer nails or screws ran through the head to strengthen the neck.

Examining the seam on the old decoy, we can see the cotton and lead white caulk that was used to seal these old blocks.

Most of these decoys were carved from Jersey white cedar and hollowed. Cedar was harvested in the winter while the sap was down. According to historian Jimmy Allen (Decoy Heritage), this prevented the sap from seeping out later and ruining the paint. Hendrickson, like many carvers of this period and region, was a boat builder, making sneak boxes ànd later PT boats during World War 2. Carvers used the same caulking methods to fill the seams of their decoys as they did to fill between the planks on their boats. Once they hollowed the two halves of a decoy, they fastened them together with either wooden dowels or small nails. Then they took soft cotton cordage saturated with thick lead white paint and pressed it between the halves with a special tool. Some carvers inserted the nails only from the top half, keeping the nail holes above the waterline. Others alternated the nails on the top and bottom around the decoy and filled the holes with some of the lead white caulk. Incredibly, the old Hendrickson black duck I have still shows the cotton and lead caulk along its seam. Thankfully, the excellent

waterproof glues and epoxies of today mean we no longer have to deal with the toxic lead.

Carvers of the Jersey Shore school used several different methods to attach their decoy heads. They might run a large nail or long screw from the top of the head and use several small finish nails around the neckline, using the lead caulk to fill the large nail hole in the top. Some carvers ran a wooden dowel down through the top of the head or up from the base of the neck and then secured the head using several smaller nails around the neck. Other carvers frowned on this method because they believed the wooden dowel would absorb water and swell, causing the head to split later. The head was never glued on because at some point it would inevitably crack and

I split open one of the test pours to show how the dovetail will hold the poured lead in place.

break and need replacing. Without X-raying my decoy, I can't tell how Gene attached the head. The best I can tell is that he used four small finish nails to attach it and possibly two long hand-cut nails running in from high on the back of the neck. He may have used a screw up through the bottom of the neck, however, as the neck is not cracked except for some small checks at the nail sites.

I patterned the decoy for this demonstration from my Gene Hendrickson decoy. The measurements are fairly accurate, but some of my construction techniques will use modern materials like epoxy glues. I was able to find 9 mm upholstery tacks for the eyes on eBay. I did a bit of research to determine just how deeply to carve the inlet to hold 5 ounces of lead for the ballast weight. An inlet ¾" wide, 3" long, and ¾" deep held 11 ounces of lead. At ½" deep, the weight dropped down to 8 ounces. At ⅜" thick, the weight was a

little less than 7 ounces. The winning thickness was ¼" thick, giving me 5 ounces on the nose. I'm sure there is a bit of variation depending on how deep the undercut dovetails are.

For this project, I started out using dry white cedar that was three feet long, two inches thick, and 6 inches wide. This included the head material. It's hard to find clean cedar where I live in North Carolina, so a few knots became issues as I worked. In the demonstration I will show you how to deal with them. Two 14" long pieces of the cedar stock are needed for the body and the remaining piece can be used to make a few heads. I usually make several heads and use the best for the decoy. Let's get started on the head.

1

Lay out your head pattern on wood that is 2" thick. Make sure you run the grain straight down the bill.

2

I use a pencil to run a line down the middle of the head cutout (1"). Then I divide those two halves into quarters, giving me four sections of ½" each. You can then trace in a top pattern like this to use as carving guides. The bill will be an inch wide.

3

I pencil in the high spot for the cheek. I use the pencil as my measuring tool and my finger as a stop, and then transfer this measurement to the other side.

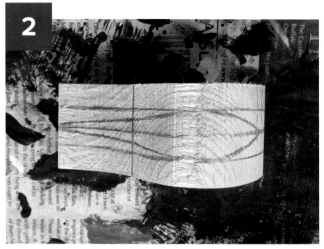

4

Most of the time I carve in the width of my bills because I like to use the knife. To save a bit of time, I use the band saw to cut up each side of the bill to the bill margin you can see on the head pattern.

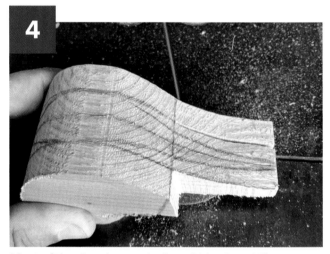

5

Using my knife, I begin rounding up the cheek where it runs into the bill on the underside of the chin. After I get it rounded into the bill and get the rest of the bill width carved, I'll repeat on the other side.

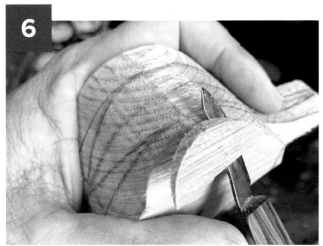

6

On the crown, I round and remove excess wood on both sides. I round down from the crown to the high spot on the cheek.

7

Moving from the crown toward the bill, I remove the excess, working from the high point on the cheek into the bill.

8

Work on both sides to keep things symmetrical and remove the excess straight into the bill.

9

Round out the back of the neck, working from the high point of the cheek to the center of the back of the neck and head. Work on both sides to ensure symmetry. The wood here will carve easiest if you work from the midpoint toward the back.

10

Work both sides up until the head looks close to this. Working on both sides a little at a time will help to keep the head symmetrical.

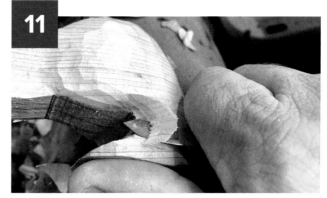

11

Begin carving out between the cheek and the base of the neck. You don't have to go too far here as you will finish the area after you've glued the head to the body.

12

A coarse round file or rasp makes getting into tight areas much easier. Here I use one to round things up around the throat area of the head.

13

Look at the head from the front, top, and back to make it symmetrical. Here you can see the neck isn't carved as deeply on one side, but that is okay for now since I will be carving the neck into the body a bit later.

14

I begin removing wood from the back of the bill to the front and from the top guideline down to the lower edge. Remove wood slowly as this area likes to split.

15

I usually leave this thickness on the end of the bill. At this point, I also draw in the bill margin where the bill meets the head. Gene Hendrickson made his margins as straight as possible. Here you can see those lines are rounded.

16

To flatten the margin line, I remove some of the fullness here. I redraw the line and look from the end of the bill, repeating the process until I like the curve.

17

This looks about right.

18

I draw in the rounded end of the bill. Carefully removing wood from both the top and bottom, I work on one side and then the other.

19

Once the curves are about the same, put the knife down and finish rounding with the sanding block. It is hard to remove too much wood accidentally with sandpaper.

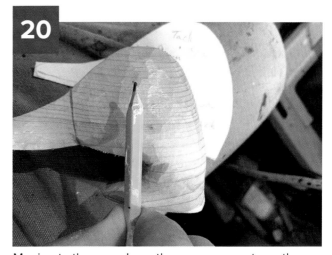

20

Moving to the eyes, I use the measurements on the pattern and transfer them to the carving. Some Jersey Shore carvers simply carved out a flattened eye channel but I prefer a V-shape.

21

This looks about right.

22

With my knife I make a stop cut straight in along the line I drew about ⅜" deep on each side. I then carve up into the stop cut to form the bottom of the eye channel.

23

I finish the eye channel by carving down from the top.

24

Work on both sides for symmetry. Feel into the channels with your fingers to help determine that they are carved evenly. Once you get them where they look and feel the same, sand them out to remove the knife marks. You can also rasp out the head and sand it at this point.

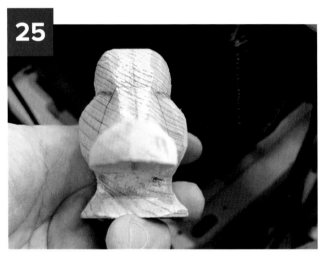

25

Look at the channels again from the front and back to ensure they look the same. Once you tack in the eyes it is hard to make corrections.

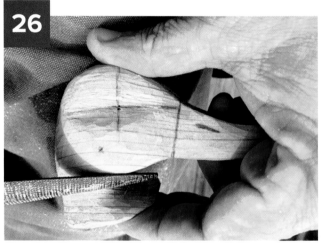

26

Using the pattern for measurements, locate the eye placement. I measure up from the base of the neck and end of the bill.

27

I press the tack eyes into place but don't set them. When they stick out, I can look from the top and front to make sure they are set evenly.

28

Once both eye locations are good, I drive the eyes all the way in. I set them so they rest flat at the base of the eye channel.

29

Turning now to the bill details, I draw in where the nostrils, the V-notch, and lower bill groove will be. Check from the front and top to get them symmetrical before you carve them in.

30

Using a small detail knife, I first cut straight down in along my lines. I then carve into those cuts from the cheek into the bill.

31

For the V-notch, I press and cut hard into the point of the V but not so deeply at the top of corner of the bill. This will taper the cut toward the top of the bill. I then cut into that cut and chip out the wood.

32

On the underside of the bill, I make a stop cut straight down into the margin line. I then cut into that cut from the underside of the head toward the bill, chipping out the wood.

33

I cut out the nostril using a small V-gouge. You can also do this with a detail knife or even by stoning it with small stoning tools/Dremel/micromotor.

35

Cut two pieces of the 2" x 6" stock to a length of 14 inches. Then draw a centerline down the length of the top and bottom of each piece.

37

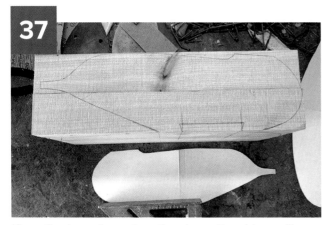

Place the two pieces together, trace the side profile on them, and again draw in the inlet location as noted on the pattern.

34

Finish the head by cutting in the detail along the bill's bottom edge. If you haven't sanded the head, do it now. The neck doesn't need to be sanded as we still have some carving to do once it is attached to the body.

36

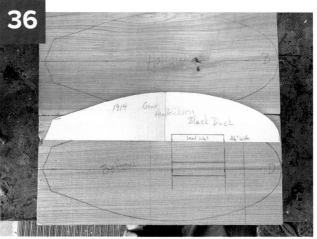

Take the top view of the pattern and trace it onto the top and bottom of each piece. I am going to use a hollowing technique that requires the pattern to be on the top and bottom of each piece. Mark out the inlet for the lead ballast on the side you want to be the very bottom.

38

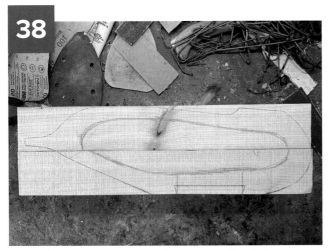

I now draw in an approximate area on the side pattern that will be a guide to how deep I can hollow out each piece of wood without making the decoy too thin in any one area.

39

I also draw approximate hollowing guide lines on the inside of each half.

40

Time to cut out the inlet. Using a ¾" flat chisel, I initiate the cuts on each end to prevent the wood from splitting down the length of the decoy. I cut in only about an ⅛" at a time to prevent any splitting. After the ends are cut in, I then cut in along the sides using a long thin knife or large flat chisel.

41

I begin to chisel out the inlet about a ⅙" to ⅛" at a time. I re-cut in the ends as I work and angle those cuts to start forming the undercut dovetail on each end.

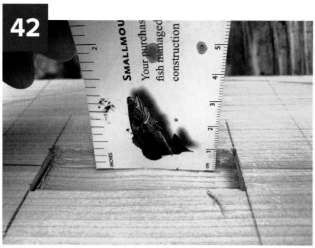

42

I work front to back and then flip back to front until I get the desired depth. Remember a 1/4" thick is about five ounces of lead once poured and 3/8" around seven ounces.

43

Time to hollow the inside of each half. Using a ¾" Forstner bit, I use the guideline on the side profile I drew to determine how deep I can drill into each half. I use a piece of painter's tape as a guide.

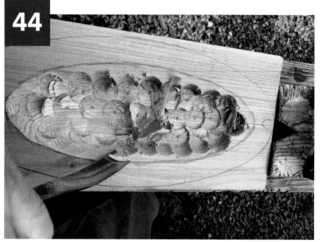

44

Once I get as much wood out as I dare with the drill and Forstner bit, I use a round gouge to neaten things up and get a little more weight out of the block. Repeat on the other half. If you accidentally remove too much wood anywhere and a hole appears when you carve, you can easily patch the area with multi-purpose Bondo.

45

Once you have each side to your liking, use the glue of your choice to attach the two pieces. I prefer two-ton epoxy to five-minute; it dries slower and allows more adjustment as the glue sets. Titebond III is also great, but takes a day to set up.

A tight seam line and some clamps will ensure that you have no air gaps in your seam once the block has dried.

After the glue has dried thoroughly, I can cut out the block. I start by making cuts on the top/bottom profile. I leave about four inches uncut near the center of the pattern on each side. This leaves the side pattern where you drew it and also leaves flat wood against your table when you do cut that side profile.

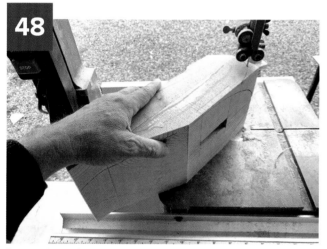

I now place the block on its side and cut out the side profile.

Placing the decoy on its bottom, I redraw the lines I cut out along the top profile by eye. I can then get back on the band saw and finish cutting out the top profile.

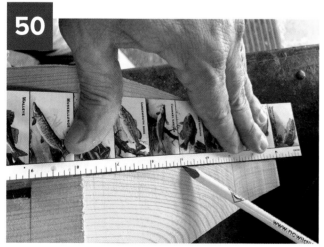

Using a flexible ruler, I redraw the centerline all the way around the decoy.

51

Place the decoy head up on the head/neck shelf and trace around the base of the neck. Looking at the original decoy, notice how a good portion of the back is fairly flat. I draw a guideline for approximating this flat area onto the block. This will let me know where I need to really round the decoy when I begin carving it.

52

Although the actual decoy bottom is rounded, there is a flat area around the weight. I draw in a guideline for this area and will round from it to the side seam lines once I begin carving.

53

Working from about the midway of the block forward, I begin rounding out from the top guidelines to the seam line on both the right and left sides of the block. Do not try to cut too far back from the midpoint or the wood will split. I use my drawknife more as a push knife and I also hold it upside down. I feel I get better depth control this way, rolling the blade on the back bevel of the edge to control the cutting depth.

54

When working on the back half of the decoy, again work from the midway to the tail. Getting too far forward will make the wood split. You can work all the way around the front and then switch to the back or work on the top and then switch to the bottom. Again, I use that guideline I drew to round from it onto the side seam line.

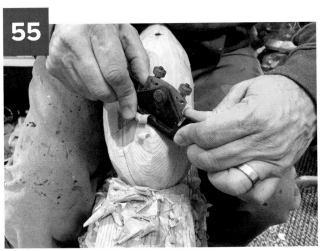

Once the block is roughly rounded, I use a spokeshave to refine the shape.

Knots are hard on your carving tools and can mess up a paint job once the sap in them begins reacting with the paint. If you are using a grinding tool to carve with, you can work right through them, but they will create problems for knives. Here I use a large drill bit or a Forstner bit the size of the knot to drill out the hard wood and get into the body about ½" to ¼" deep.

Using some of the clean scrap wood, I cut a few rectangular blocks that are slightly larger on the ends than the knot holes. I let the grain run the length of the plug. I then round out the plug with my knife, removing wood a little at a time to insure it fits and seats at the bottom of the hole. Once you have a good fit, secure it with the glue of your choice.

Once the glue sets, trim the plug flat with a small saw. Notice that I twisted the plug when it was glued up so the grain looks like it is running the same way as the decoy block. This will show a bit once the decoy is finished and painted. This plug will now carve much like the rest of the decoy.

59

I give the whole decoy a good rasping now before attaching the head. A mild sanding is also good, or rub it down well with a metal scrape. A nearly finished block reveals any carving irregularities much better than a rough block, and these are easier to correct while the head is off.

60

Time to attach the head. I mix up a small batch of five-minute epoxy and place a generous amount on the head shelf and then I place the head and center it using the guidelines I drew on the decoy and head. Wipe off excess glue as it runs out of the joint.

61

After about 30 minutes, the glue has cured enough so I can trim away the excess glue and then shape and carve the neck into the body. I rotate the body around in my hands to make sure the lines flow nicely from the neck into the body all the way around the bird.

62

A 4" or longer decking screw will strengthen the neck and hopefully prevent the head from cracking and breaking off.

63

I use a drill bit the same size as the screw head and drill into the back of the head, just deep enough to hide the screw. I then run in a tap hole using a small drill bit slightly smaller than the shaft diameter of the screw. This will prevent the screw from splitting the head when I screw it in.

64

Once I've run the screw into the head, I fill the hole with some epoxy wood. When that sets, I carve and sand it down to the shape of the back of the head.

65

Time to give the tail a bit of attention. I am really surprised at how thin the original decoys' tails are, many being only about an ⅛" thick. I use a sharp, thin-bladed knife to carve in the transition from the body into the tail. I find a longer blade works well as you can put pressure on the blade as you carve to bend it somewhat to make the needed cuts.

66

Once you've established the thickness of the tail, you can trim the length and shape it the way you want it. Some carvers left the tail flat, some rounded it off, and some carved it to a point.

67

Get a lead melting pot going in a well-ventilated area and wear eye protection. While the lead is heating up, I use a small level and a few wedges of wood to level the decoy's inlet. We left that area flat for a reason. Once the lead is ready, I pour it in so it is level with the surface of the inlet. Let the lead set up and cool off.

68

For some finishing touches, I burn my brand deep into the bottom and I also use a punch set to add my initials and the year.

69

Finish the carving part of the decoy by rasping out any rough areas and then give it a thorough sanding. I use 120-grit for my final sanding. I then seal the decoy with two coats of spar urethane, sanding between coats.

PAINTING AND FINISHING

Looking over hundreds of photographs and going through my decoy books showed me that the paint on the puddle ducks from this region of New Jersey were almost always very simple. The Barnegat/Jersey Shore black ducks were about as simple as they came. The hand-carved working blocks usually had tan heads with nearly black bodies. A black crown and stripe over the eye and maybe a bit of purple or green for the speculum finished off the bird. The brown on the body was so dark that it may as well have been pure black. I remember how, in the class I mentioned earlier, Jamie Hand mixed up a can of paint for the class to use. He took a quart can of oil-based flat black Ronan, took a small tube of artist brown oil paint, mixed that into the black with a brush…and that was it. The paint looked pretty much like pure black unless you held it against real pure black, and then maybe you could imagine just a slight difference.

That was it for the basic black duck. However, many carvers back in the day would go a step further and create a "deluxe" paint job by quickly scratching in loops through the wet paint on the body to suggest body feathers. Using a nail, the end of a paint brush, or some other blunt object, they would start near the head and work their way to the tail end of the decoy, scratching off the wet paint in a fish-scale or looping pattern. This would reveal the lighter primed or even bare wood underneath. There is a good interview with Harry V. Shourds II as he paints one of his black ducks in this manner on a Folkstreams film/video by Louis Presti called In the Barnegat Bay Tradition online. I encourage you to find and watch the video. Near the 22-minute mark Shourds shows exactly how to do the scratch painting. Even though the feather and paint pattern was rough and didn't look like much, an old bird today with the scratch paint still in good shape is much more collectible than one with the very basic paint pattern.

There were also some variations in the detail work on the heads among many of the old-school carvers. As mentioned, for the most part the head paint was simply tan with a black crown and stripe running through the eye. The bills usually had an olive-green tone. Some carvers would go a step further and splatter fine black onto the head to suggest the ticking black ducks have. Other carvers would stipple in the fine black specks with the end of a blunt bristle brush, while others would use a fine detail brush to paint in the ticking. Some of the Gene Hendrickson blacks I've seen had the fine ticks painted in as simple short horizontal lines all over the head.

A few carvers would go even further and scratch paint the ticking on the head, first priming the head with the dark brown or black. Once that dried, the painter added tan and, while that was still wet, he would scratch the ticking in to reveal the darker paint underneath the tan.

I'll demonstrate some of these techniques but let you decide on the amount of detail you want to put on your birds. They hunt great and don't take up a lot of time to make, so have fun with the demonstration.

These decoys were traditionally painted with oils. For this project I'm going to use Parker Decoy Paint. (Parker actually makes a black duck decoy kit: www. parkercoatings.com/decoy.html. The smallest can sizes are plenty to do a dozen or so decoys.) I use slightly different colors than what they include in the kit since this is a very traditional paint pattern. I use the #3 brown for the body. It is very dark, almost black. #30 river bottom is the tan I like, and the head will also need #5 black. The bill will be #11 green gold. This color is perfect for both mallard drakes and black ducks. If you want to add some color for the speculum, consider their #69 blue or #64 purple.

I put two coats of the tan on the head. I use the neck/body seam line as a guideline. Once this paint dries, I can make it age and get an instant patina by buffing the paint quickly with a piece of brown paper bag. Since the paint hasn't fully cured, the paper will distress the paint a bit but will also add a bit of shine. This step is optional.

Parker Paints are fairly thin and require two coats of each color. They are very durable and dry very flat. I first paint the body with two coats of brown, letting the paint dry between coats.

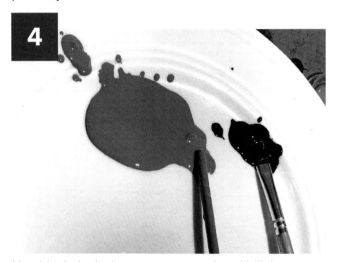

Hen black ducks have a greener colored bill than drakes. This will be a hen, so I use a bit of green oil paint I already had on hand. Any green will work as long as it is oil based. I mix just a few drops of the green with the Parker green gold.

5

I add two coats of the green gold to the bill.

6

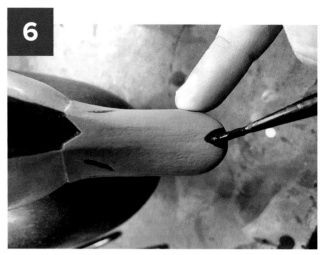

Once the green gold has dried, I use black to paint in a bill nail.

7

While the brush has black on it, I paint the crown.

8

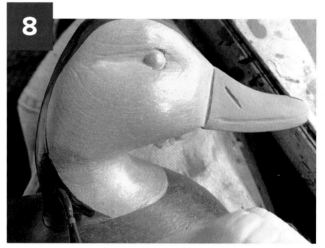

This black moves all the way down the back of the neck and curves to the front of the neck. Repeat this on both sides of the head and neck.

9

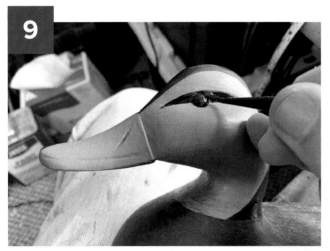

I add the eye stripe, curving from about the front of the bill to the back of the neck. They eye is also black. Put a second coat of black everywhere you need it.

10

Most traditional carvers would call this paint job done here, but I'll go a few steps further just to spruce it up a bit.

11

Some carvers would scratch through the tan paint to a darker underpaint for the ticking. Here I first paint the head black and let it dry thoroughly. I then paint over the black with my tan and use a sharpened piece of bamboo chopstick while the tan paint is still wet to scratch in my ticking. Clean off the removed paint often from your scratch tool.

13

Stripes about two inches long look to be about right for this bird. I add two coats of the purple. Once the paint dries, the hand-painted lines will look accurate for the project. If I had taped off the speculum for the paint, the sharp edges may look out of place with the rest of the hand-painted decoy.

15

12

From what I've seen, only a few of the old Jersey black duck carvers would paint speculums. I like them, so mine is going to have them. I use a piece of 1" painter's tape to decide the angle and where the speculum is going to be. I then use a white colored pencil to lightly draw in the outline of the tape and size it accordingly. The tape allows me to change the angles and locations of the speculum on both sides before committing to paint. I look from above to see I have both sides about the same.

14

That is all I need for the painting. Once the bird dries, I can again buff the surface some more with the brown paper bag to get the shine where I want it. Or you can just leave the flat finish as is.

Our final step is to add a leather line tie on the bottom in front of the inlet. I use a strip of old leather belt and a few 1¼" brass nails for the job. I try to drive the nails in slightly out of line of each other to the wood grain in the decoy. This will help prevent placing too much stress in one spot, which could split the grain over time.

OLD-SCHOOL DECOYS

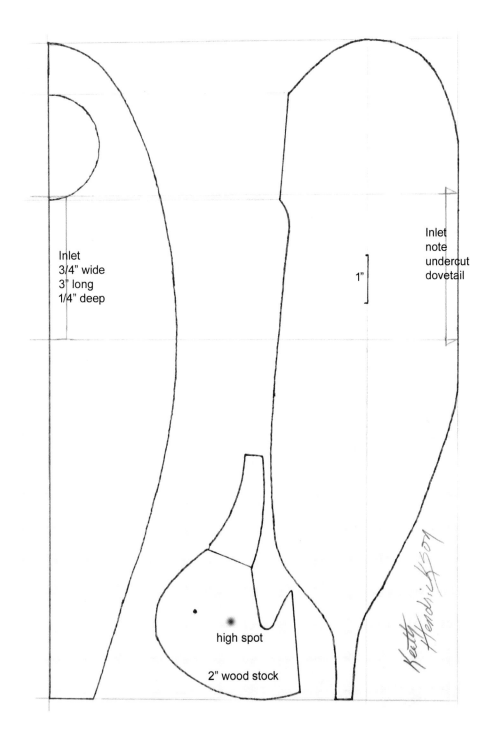

Inlet
3/4" wide
3" long
1/4" deep

Inlet
note
undercut
dovetail

1"

high spot

2" wood stock

**Barnegat Bay Black Duck (50% life-size)
pattern by Keith Hendrickson**

CORK BLACK DUCK

It was mid-January on a small pothole just off Coinjock Bay in Currituck, North Carolina. In the early-morning darkness I discovered that the decoy bag that was supposed to be in my stick blind wasn't there. But I found a lone, nearly rotten cork black duck decoy in some leaves and debris under the bench seat. It had no weights, but I rummaged through my shell box and found a piece of cord about 3 feet long. I waded out into the pond and shoved a long stick into the mud, and then tied the decoy to it. As a sliver of orange appeared in the eastern sky, I heard wings and then a splash. The old decoy was no longer alone. I was amazed how this one cork bird pulled in a quick limit of teal, mallards, and black ducks all by itself without any calling.

I'm sure many duck hunters have heard similar stories about using a single block to pull in decoy-shy birds late in the season. I have used this technique many times since with great success, and I still use it often when hunting small ponds and potholes. No wonder the old salts handed this trick down to new duck hunters.

A black duck is one of my go-to birds for gifts or donations because it is fairly easy to carve and the paint can be as simple as you want. It's also a great first bird for a new carver. I drafted one of my students, Jonathan Maulden, to carve this decoy out of high-density cork. Jonathan began hunting in 2008 and started carving with me last winter. He is a very quick learner and is currently working to convert his hunting rig into all wood-and-cork blocks.

We used high density cork for this demonstration because it is easy to work with just a few basic hand tools. It is also dense enough so you don't need a bottom or tail board, provided you leave some beef in the tail. It is also easy to paint with just a handful of colors. Although this demonstration bird uses a cork body, you can substitute any lightweight wood of your preference. The pattern pulls its influence from the New Jersey shore with a touch of Ward Brothers' style in the head, giving the block some old-school glamour.

TOOLS/MATERIALS

- Block of high density cork measuring 15" L x 6" W x 4" D

- Wood head stock of your choice measuring at least 6" x 4" x 2" thick. I like clean white pine, basswood, or white cedar.

- 5-minute epoxy, Apoxie Sculpt, and/or QuikWood epoxy putty

- 1 pair 10 mm dark brown glass eyes and a 10 mm drill bit

- About 10 inches of ⅜" hardwood dowel and an extra-long ⅜" drill bit

- Carving knives or rotary carving tool

- Coarse and fine wood rasps or Stanley Surform rasp.

- Cork sealer or spar varnish/urethane

- Paint: flat black, white, tan, and Van Dyke brown paints of your choice. I like Ronan oils or BEHR latex. Small amounts of yellow ochre, raw sienna, and purple are used for the bill and wing speculums and I'll use tube paints for these—oils for the Ronan and acrylics for the latex.

We begin by laying out the top view of the pattern onto the top of the 6" x 15" high-definition cork block. Mark your centerline and then trace the pattern onto the block, flipping the pattern to get both halves.

Now flip the cork onto its side and trace the side view of the pattern on the block. Make sure the front of the pattern matches up with the front of the top view you already traced onto the block.

3

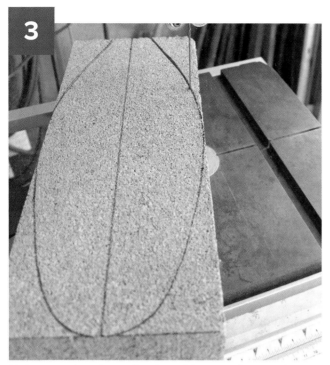

Using your band saw, begin cutting out the top view but cut ONLY partially towards the center on each side and each end. You want to leave about four inches of the middle of your traced lines uncut so you have some secure flat block left to support the cork when you place it on its side to cut out the side view. When you make this partial cut, you can slightly pry out each corner of the cork away from your saw blade to relieve any pressure the cork may be creating against the blade, so you can back the saw blade out of the cork to make your next cut.

5

Now flip the block back onto its bottom and finish cutting out the sections of the top view you left intact. You can draw in new lines if need help to guide your cutting.

4

With the four corners still attached to the block, flip it onto the side and cut out the side profile.

6

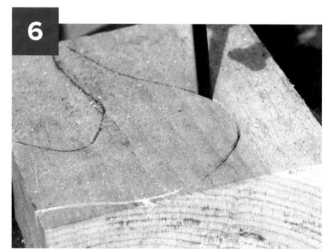

Trace the head pattern onto the side of your head wood stock. You want the grain to run the length of the bill into the head to keep the bill from breaking. If you have a drill press you can drill a ¼-inch pilot hole all the way through the block for the eye location. This will put the eyes in the same spots on each side of the head and make future steps much easier. If you don't have a drill press, you can align the eyes while carving the head.

With the head cut out, we will begin carving. Draw a centerline all the way around the head and trace in the approximate width of the bill and top view of the head using the pattern for reference. Clamp the head into a vise and remove excess wood from the bill and sides of the head. We use a drawknife but any rotary tool will work, too. Try to remove the same amount of wood from both sides to keep the head fairly symmetrical. This is easier to do if you switch from side to side instead of working on just one side at a time.

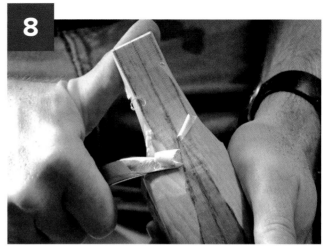

Once you've removed the bulk of the wood, use a carving knife or rotary tool to fine tune your carving. Work from side to side and look at the head from the top, front, and back to get the head as symmetrical as possible. Carve out any flat areas and leave a common high spot on each cheek. For the base of the neck, simply round off the corners and leave some to carve after you place the head on the body.

Locate the approximate eye location on each side of the head using the side and top patterns. If you drilled in your eye, you've done this already. Your pencil is a great tool to keep things on track. Use it constantly to replace any lines you carve out as you work.

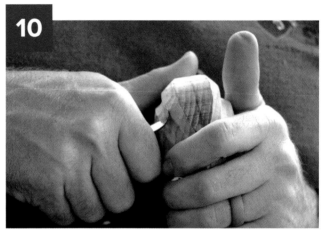

Carve in the eye channels to approximately the width of the bill where the top of the bill meets the head on your pattern. Here we use a bent blade carving knife, but you can simply cut a V-channel with a straight knife or use a rotary tool.

11

Switching over to the body, draw in the centerline all the way around. Also, place the roughed-out head in place and trace around the base of the neck, making sure it's centered in the proper location.

12

Use a small block of wood as a guide (we use another head cutout that is about 1.75 inches thick) and trace a waterline chine 1.75 inches high around the side of the body. Simply place a pen or pencil on the block and rotate it around the body.

13

Flip the decoy onto the bottom and draw a bottom oval ring around the base that is about an inch to an inch and a half in from the sides of the decoy. Let the oval ring extend all the way to the front and back of your cutout. This ring doesn't have to be exact, but try and make it symmetrical for the right and left halves.

14

Now we begin carving the cork block. Remove the excess cork with a drawknife or even a small sheetrock saw or bread knife. You want to carve the top of the block from the centerline, rounding down to that chine line we drew in around the sides of the decoy. Round the bottom of the decoy from the oval ring on the bottom of the bird up to the side chine line. Leave the tail full for strength. Be careful not to carve into the head shelf where the neck will attach.

Once the body is roughed out, refine the carving with a wood rasp or Stanley Surform. Again, work from side to side and front to back to remain symmetrical.

You can refine further with a fine rasp or sandpaper.

Look at the decoy from the front, back, top, and bottom, to make sure it is as symmetrical as you can make it. Round out any flat areas. The only flat areas that should remain is the oval bottom of the decoy and the head shelf.

Here you can see how we rounded down from the centerline on top of the back to the side chine, and from the oval bottom up. If you want wing indentions at the tail, you can carve these in with a rounded rasp or file.

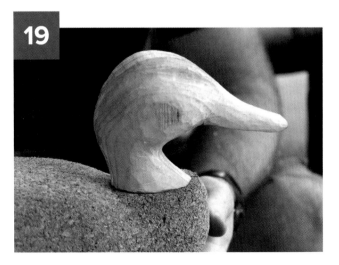

Begin carving the neck into the body. Refine the shape of the neck on the head and then begin rounding the breast of the block to match the angles on the neck.

20

Redraw any lines you carve out.

21

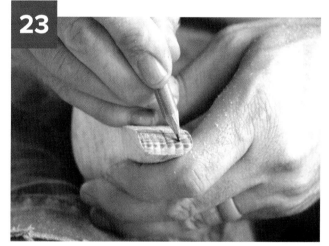

Finish carving out the head shelf where the neck and body meet.

22

With the head resting in place, the neck should flow into the breast with no sharp angular changes.

23

Switching attention back to the head, rasp and sand down the head and round off the end of the bill. This is best done by first drawing in some guidelines so you can make sure you round the bill evenly.

24

Draw in the approximate bill margins where the bill meets the head. You will need this to get the proper eye location if you didn't drill a guide hole for the eyes earlier. The next few steps will show you how to get eyes that look right once the head is finished. Note that many old decoys didn't use eyes, so you may want to skip these steps altogether.

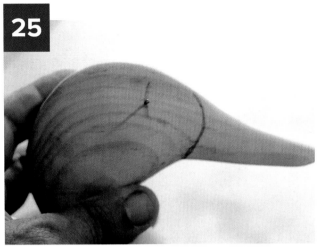

25

Using your pattern, locate the approximate location of the eye and press in a pushpin or a small finish nail on one side of the head.

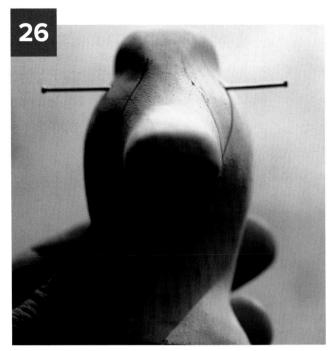

26

Place another pin on the other side of the head, and look from the front and top to make sure the pins line up.

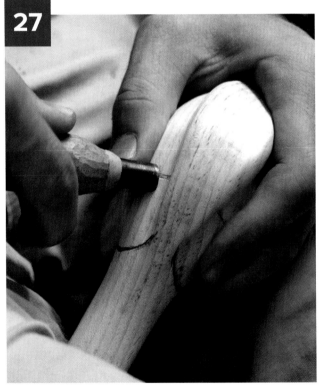

27

Remove the pins and drill a 10 mm hole about ¼- to ½-inch deep, centering the hole on each pin location. Drill each hole so it is angled slightly forward. Here we are using a tool made from a spent brass gun cartridge that was inserted into a piece of broom handle. Sharpen the edge of the cartridge with a fine file or sandpaper. Press the tool into the wood with a twisting motion. Then you can remove the inner wood from the cut by chipping it out with a knife.

28

The eye channels should hit the center of the eye hole. Refine your eye channels where needed, making the depth of the channel meet the bill margin.

29

Using a rotary tool or sandpaper, round out the eye socket holes so there are no sharp edges where the holes meet the eye channels.

30

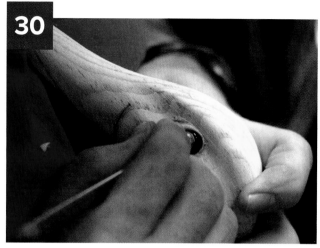

We begin setting the eyes by cutting off a small section of QuikWood epoxy and mixing it together. Once the putty is well kneaded and mixed, fill each eye socket. Press a glass eye into each socket with the eraser end of your pencil.

31

The eyes should be set deep enough into the sockets so they do not look bug-eyed. You want to see just a bit of each eye from the top. Use your eraser to move the eyes forward or back so they are symmetrical from the top. You want them to appear like they are angled slightly forward.

32

From the front, the eyes should be level and in the same location on the head. They should not be angled up.

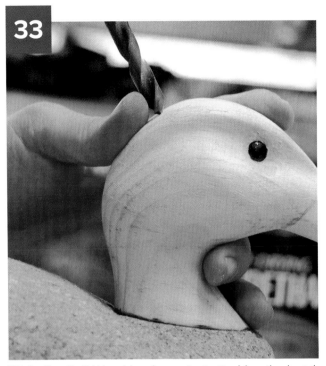

33

While the QuikWood hardens, start attaching the head to the body. First, glue on the head with 5-minute epoxy. Once the epoxy sets, use the extra-long ⅜" bit to drill a hole from the top of the head well into the cork body. Start the bit at a 90-degree angle to the top of the head so it doesn't want to slide down the head. Once you start the hole, you can change the approach so it angles to the bottom of the decoy. You want to come close to the centerline of your decoy.

35

If we wanted a keel, we would drill a hole through the keel and into the body and insert another piece of the ⅜" dowel. But since we are going to use a flat weight, we use a Forstner bit to drill a larger diameter hole and glue in a small piece of broom handle. Then we sand the handle flush with the bottom of the decoy. We will screw our weight to this.

34

We decided not to use a keel on this decoy since we will use it as a carry-in bird on small potholes. A small flat weight will let the decoy self-right, but also allow slight breezes to give it a bit more action on the water. We are going to use a leather line tie, so we angle our ⅜" drill hole so it emerges from the lower rounded area of the breast. We then coat a dowel with epoxy and insert it into the hole. (If we had used a keel, we would have glued it on before drilling the hole. Then we would have drilled the hole straight down and into the keel.) Once the epoxy hardens, we cut off the end of the dowel and sand it. The bottom end of the dowel will serve as the anchor point for the screw that will secure the leather tie line tab.

36

Once the QuikWood is set securely behind the eyes, mix a small amount of Apoxie Sculpt and make a pea-sized ball. Press this ball over the eye.

37

Wet your thumb and fingers and swipe over the eye, using a good bit of pressure. A small amount of Apoxie will get pressed away and removed as you swipe. Just swipe back and forth and the eyelid shape will begin to form itself. Remove as much Apoxie as necessary, smoothing as you go.

38

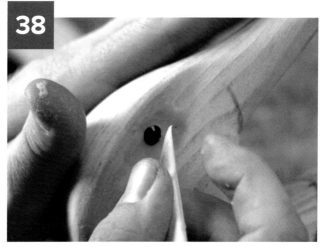

Finish forming the eyelid with a plastic sculpting tool or a toothpick. You can even carve your own sculpting tools from wooden chopsticks. Don't use anything that can scratch the glass eyes.

39

The finished eyes should have a natural look and both sides should match. Allow the Apoxie Sculpt to harden thoroughly.

40

You can sand your bird or leave the cork a bit rough to make it appear flatter on the water. Seal the bird using cork sealer, spar varnish, or spar urethane. I like to put about three coats of sealer on a bird I know will be hunted over, allowing ample time for each coat to dry. This block is going to get painted with oils, so a thinned coat of flat black Ronan oil will serve as a primer. If you use latex paint, prime the decoy with a coat of toned Kilz Professional Latex that has bonding chemicals in the paint. Here we let Jonathan's little helper, Ethan, apply the paint. It is always great to start them young!

41

We use full-strength Van Dyke brown to paint the body. If you don't have that color, you can mix raw umber and black to make an appropriate dark brown.

42

The head is painted tan. You can mix this color from raw sienna, white, and a bit of your brown.

43

Once the tan on the head has dried, use a large bristle brush to stipple in a touch of black across the crown and even a bit all over the cheeks. This is almost a dry brush technique. Lay a small amount of paint onto a plate and barely dab the ends of the brush bristles into the paint. Then lightly dab the tips of the brush onto the surface of the head.

44

Paint the eye stripes down the middle of the eye channels. It is okay to paint right over the top of the eye.

45

The bill is a dark mustard brown for drakes and a pale olive green for hens. To mix this yellow, I use some yellow ochre, white, and a drop or three of black. For the green, I mix a bit of forest green to these same colors. If using tube oils, use a drop of Japan Dryer to speed up the drying time.

46

Once the bill has dried, line the edge with a fine round brush. Use black to paint on the nostrils and nail.

47

If you want to add a bit of color to your decoy, paint in the wing speculums. Take the time to draw them on first with a pencil. Measure carefully to get them the same size and in the same spot on each side. For this black duck, we use purple tube oils mixed with a bit of white to lighten the purple up where it can be seen over the dark brown paint.

48

Once the painting is done, clean off the eyes with either a wooden toothpick or the sharpened end of a bamboo chopstick. Carefully scrape all the excess dried paint off each eye.

49

The finished bird is handsome enough to rest on any mantle as is with its flat bare bottom. Our bird will get a flat puck-style weight to make it float properly. The leather tie line will finish off the decoy. The pattern not only makes a great black duck, but it can also serve as a hen or drake mallard if you want to get fancier with your paints. You can certainly round off the tail more if desired, but make sure it stays fairly thick since the pattern doesn't call for using a tail board. Let me warn you about giving one of these away as a present. Once people see this decoy, everyone will want one—or a dozen!

Cork Black Duck (50% life-size) - pattern by Keith Hendrickson

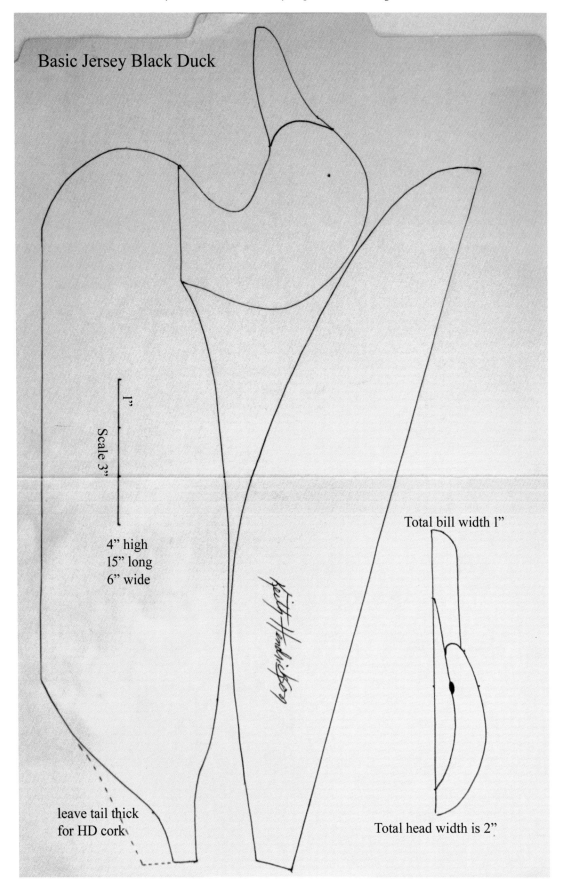

Basic Jersey Black Duck

1"

Scale 3"

4" high
15" long
6" wide

leave tail thick
for HD cork

Total bill width 1"

Total head width is 2"